Sister Mary

A story of a healing relationship

Sister Mary

A story of a healing relationship

Nini Herman LMSSA
Psychotherapist

Whurr Publishers Ltd
London

© 1999 Whurr Publishers
First published 1999 by
Whurr Publishers Ltd
19b Compton Terrace, London N1 2UN, England

British Library Cataloguing in Publication Data
A catalogue record for this book is available from the British
Library.

ISBN 1 86156 117 2

Printed and bound in the UK by Athenaeum Press Ltd,
Gateshead, Tyne & Wear

For Dr Paula Fernandes,
For Mother General
And, as always, for Dr Sydney Klein

Contents

It could be that the slowness of psychotherapy is not only due to the inherent difficulty of the problem, but also the possibility that our psychodynamic interpretations have been missing something vital. Everything in a given field cannot be seen from one point of view, and often a change of viewpoint leads to a deeper understanding.

Harry Guntrip (1977). 'Schizoid phenomena, object relations and the self'. *International Psycho-analytical Library*, 77, p. 171.

Obedience keeps the rules. Love knows when to break them.

Anthony de Nella. *One Minute Wisdom*. Image Books, New York.

It is never too late to have a happy childhood.

Attributed to Bruno Bettelheim.

Preface

Sister Mary came to me for help, with the blessing of Mother General. She was then in her mid-forties. In these pages she tells her own story in such moving detail that few words are needed to introduce her.

Herself a twin, one of five children, she had a happy start to life in Ireland, until the breakdown of her mother plunged the family into painful disarray. It was then, when she was six or seven years old, that her much-loved and admired father, unable to cope without his wife's presence and support, turned into the sexual abuser of his daughter, of little Mary. The story of the first incident of abuse Mary sets out in simple terms, the like of which has scarcely appeared in the literature on the subject.

In later chapters she describes her three years of analytical psychotherapy with myself, which included, exceptionally, a phase of art therapy at a time when she was almost mute. We read how, little by little, from being a suicidal 'frozen scrap', she shook off the role of the victim – of a murderous little girl in hiding – to take possession joyfully of the 'open road' of her life.

I came to psychotherapy as my chosen way of life after two decades of work as a family doctor in the National Health Service. During those years it dawned on me that most of my time was, mysteriously, taken up by a relatively small number of the patients on my 'list', but that I simply lacked the skill to help them extricate themselves from a malaise I came to recognise as my own. Its main symptom, to put it in a nutshell, could be described as a baffling stalemate in one's life, an angry frustration and sense of envy that others seemed to know where they were going, and despair of any remedy. Sister Mary was such a patient when she and I first got together.

Introduction

This book came into being out of a drawn-out struggle to integrate three themes, which were interrelated because they grew out of my work with one patient. Their outline will be set out here to clarify what follows.

The initial intention was to share a heartfelt celebration, a thanksgiving in effect, for Sister Mary's remarkable recovery from sexual abuse in childhood. She had come to me lost in an inner wilderness, to emerge from her fearsome tunnel into a light of day few might have anticipated.

From this transpired the second purpose, to instil hope that help was possible into the prison camps of victims, who are living trapped and blighted lives that often seem scarcely worth struggling on with and not infrequently lead to suicide. It need hardly be said that the nightmare of sexual abuse – incest in the case of Sister Mary – has been swept under the carpet of denial for inexcusable lengths of time to compound the suffering, where secrecy leads to tragic isolation for the violated while the perpetrators go free.

Lastly, I decided to once again put my professional self on the line, and not for the first time, by setting out how in the course of this therapeutic journey we deviated at times from the classical 'technique'.[1] First, art therapy – of which more later on – was introduced (resorted to might be a better term) at a stage when the patient was so inhibited in speaking as to be virtually mute. Second, on occasion I responded to Sister Mary's needs intuitively, more as a friend than as one who goes about her 'business as a psychotherapist' while much of the work followed classical lines.

The 'silent patient' is, of course, nothing new. Where the time-span for a given treatment promises to be open-ended it will, as a

---

[1] Nini Herman (1988). My Kleinian Home. London: Free Association Books.

rule, be possible, not unlike attending a woman in labour, to patiently await developments.

But here, the gift of time, as of a second weekly session, came somewhat piecemeal. A posting of my patient overseas was ever in the wings; we were not to know that, little by little, we would, by the generosity of Mother General, be granted repeated extensions that finally added up to a lease of three-and-a-quarter years.

To publish, to 'come clean', with such a controversial approach is likely to be viewed as scandalous. Colleagues will see it as 'crossing boundaries', as 'acting in' or 'acting out' an unforgivable offence that carries grave opprobrium for anyone who queers that pitch, as the precedents have shown.

Further, since I underwent a long, 'orthodox' Kleinian analysis over a total of some 15 years, from which I derived the greatest measure of benefit, it feels almost churlish, ungrateful or rebellious to 'kick over the traces'. It must be how a Catholic priest feels on entering a love relationship with a woman, and surely says something about the dubious power wielded by any fundamentalism that clouds the healthy flexibility that dwells in the open heart.

For all my love of psychoanalysis, greater is my love for the freedom to follow the drum of my heart since, from my earliest years, this fidelity alone rescued me from sinking entirely in the quicksands of obliterated existence. Looking back over a quarter of a century of clinical practice as a psychotherapist I can confirm how this primary allegiance and trust must have loosened and then untied the knots and strictures of my training little by little, to the benefit, as I see it, of my patients to heal – a word that is sadly absent from the psychoanalytic literature.

Here, in all fairness, let it be said that although my analyst himself never side-stepped from his classical approach he never failed to encourage my chosen pathways, saying 'you are not an analyst but a psychotherapist'. I decided, on reflection, to give this utterance the benefit of the doubt, that it could, knowing the unfailing probity of the man, be taken in the most creative and liberating way.[2]

It is important, however, to remind ourselves that psychoanalytical psychotherapy is the child of a stern parent discipline that is now, as is the way with generations, increasingly striking out to forge its own identity as it questions the nature of the input that nourishes the

---

[2] Psychoanalysts are, by definition, trained with the Institute of Psychoanalysis. This is seen as ensuring, or trying to ensure, personal stability and a certain level of skill as prerequisites for working under that designation. In reality it ensures neither because this is not possible.

roots of healing. For, as Harry Guntrip put it[3], 'what is to be done with what becomes conscious?'

No one likes to be in the wilderness. For this reason I call to my defence in Part One two famous predecessors who broke 'the rules'. The first was Freud, the second Winnicott. Rules revolve around what is known as 'technique', surely an unfortunate term to define the nature of a relationship perhaps unequalled in its scope for human intimacy.

I was no novice to art therapy, having 'supervised' a remarkably gifted team of art therapists in the psychiatric hospital in west London where I worked for a number of years. If 'supervision' was my official function, I was in fact a humble apprentice to its undoubted efficacy in reaching patients who were scarcely accessible to words – many were mute – in their straitjacket of body language.

Small groups of these lost souls, who were escorted from the 'back wards' for their session, would be settled down at a table and given a subject to illustrate or, at other times, left to their own devices. In either case, the work that resulted after, say, half an hour would often reveal a dazzling insight into the chaos of their inner world, and they were able to respond with gestures, sometimes even with bursts of language, to the therapist's interpretations – however tentative they inevitably had to be at times.

If I initially harboured certain doubts with regard to the process these were entirely dispelled when, in the course of a lunch hour, I was invited to 'have a go'. Free to choose my own subject I was startled at what emerged. Here was a drawing of a man in a black coat and hat, clearly respectable, fleeing from a burning city. Asked to comment on my production, tears running down my face, I recognised my father, leaving Germany in a great hurry, on the day that Hitler was voted Reichschancellor. The scene must, in my mind, have been associated with the Sunday on which the Reichstag burned when I was six or seven years of age.[4]

Accordingly, when I suggested to Sister Mary that she might help us along if she tried to paint, she took to this with instant enthusiasm. This work, carried out in her spare time, gave us access to her tormented inner world to a degree that might have taken many more years to get a glimpse of, let alone to obtain, such compelling, vivid pictures. Furthermore, although she had, during the first phase of

---

[3] Harry Guntrip (1977). 'Schizoid phenomena, object relations and the self'. *International Psycho-analytical Library*. The Hogarth Press and the Institute of Psycho-Analysis, London, p. 355.

[4] The Reichstag was the German Parliament; then still a bastion of democracy.

our work together, rather tended to scoff at any notion of a deeper level of her mind – of the unconscious – she now became a firm believer and began to take pleasure in working to further the understanding that would presently set her free.

Art therapy began in Germany around the time when Freud was making his first discoveries in the course of treating women diagnosed as suffering from hysteria. The psychiatrist who set the ball rolling had no idea that these works could give access to the wandering mind. Trained initially as an art historian, he admired the creations in their own artistic right and, indeed, parts of his collection were shown in the Hayward Gallery while I was working on this introduction.[5] Further, by another of those coincidences to which some attribute all manner of spooky conspiracies, at the same time my eye caught an article in *The Independent* which carried a large, brightly coloured painting that seemed familiar somehow. Paying closer attention, I read that a local authority was using art therapy in the treatment of child victims of sexual abuse: a brave beginning that will hopefully grow.[6]

Likewise, the work that Freud began, not so long ago in the history of ideas, came to fruition little by little, yet at tremendous speed, as the result of an inspired groping in the dark. An approach that often worked by accident rather than by design created a jumping-off board for the next 'experiment' which followers used in their turn as an established way to proceed. Sadly, this edifice, which grew with such spontaneity and mounting excitement, congealed into something of a dogma best defined perhaps when we read these lines from an analyst regarded as something of 'the horse's mouth' at the time of writing:

No one should consider that any aspect of the benefit that patients receive from psychoanalysis should arise as an emanation from the person of the analyst other than his analytic function, i.e. his presiding over the psychoanalytic process.[7]

This, from a then training analyst, stands as a piece of the purest nonsense, since emanation must include the disposition of the unconscious. This notion was propagated at the time, and trainees in

---

[5] Beyond Reason. Art and Psychosis. Works from the Prinzhorn Collection. The Hayward Gallery, January to February 1997.
[6] Glenda Cooper. The drawings from hell that help to heal the trauma. *The Independent* 12 December 1996, p. 9. Account of work with victims of abuse at the NSPCC Centre for the Child at Warrington, Cheshire.
[7] Donald Meltzer (1967/79). *The Psycho-analytical Process*. Clunie Press, Perthshire, Scotland, p. 79.

supervision went into positive contortions in the work they presented in order to qualify – certainly speaking for myself.

Freud, the master, on the other hand, was clearly ambivalent, for in Volume 12 of his Collected Works we come across evidence that true creativity learns to keep open house.[8] Accordingly we read:

Young and eager psycho-analysts will no doubt be tempted to bring their own individuality freely into the discussion ... Experience does not speak in favour of an affective technique of this kind ... [which] I have no hesitation in condemning as incorrect.

However, Freud, the pioneer, then had second thoughts, for on the next page this fundamentalist approach was set aside:

... I think I am well advised however to call these rules 'recommendations' and not to claim my unconditional acceptance for them ... a course of action that is usually mistaken may, once in a while lead to the desired end.

Winnicott, rightly in my view, saw 'technique' as the analyst's defence against his patient, whereas Harry Guntrip, an analysand of his, already an analyst of high standing and used to Winnicott's inspired spontaneity, shared his distress on returning from a lecture tour in the United States:

I feel a sense of horror at finding here in psychoanalysis the same 'closed shop', dogmatic, authoritarian schools as I came up against in theology and the church. I feel this is death to progress.[9]

Dogma sadly grew subsequent to the inspired progress made by Melanie Klein to instil fanatical adherence in her band of followers. Her concepts grew out of her work with small children who could not free associate. She initiated a method of providing them with a large variety of small toys and other play materials, the child's manipulation of which offered clear pathways to the unconscious. How could dogma, technique and formality win the day in a play-room at times flooded with water, or strewn with sand in the midst of mummy and daddy dolls mutilated by every possible means in the drama of despairing attacks?

---

[8] Sigmund Freud (1913). *The Standard Edition of the Complete Psychological Works of Sigmund Freud.* Volume 12. *Papers on Technique. 1911-1915. Recommendations to Physicians Practising Psycho-Analysis.* Hogarth Press, London, pp.117–18.

[9] Jeremy Hazell (1996). *H. J. S. Guntrip; A Psychoanalytical Biography.* Free Association Books, London & New York, p.284.

Yet, in a passionate defence of her new and therefore startling ideas, which were held to be sacrilegious by 'pure' Freudians, this woman of genius, who had sprung from a background as a disgruntled housewife and less-than-perfect mother, attacked each and every deviationist as ferociously as Freud had done in his time.

Today, 'how is it to be done' is occupying – at times one might almost say tormenting – a growing number of therapists whose own analysis and training followed orthodox, dogmatic lines. I no longer doubt that, since patients generally had parents who suffered from an incapacity to love fearlessly and demonstrably, commonly through generations, let alone parents who abused a child psychologically or sexually by trampling all over their potential for healthy development and growth, such victims will need more than 'interpretations' and 'insights' if they are to crawl out of hiding. Sadly, the psychoanalytic community in my experience, with notable exceptions, is hardly an advertisement for simple open-heartedness – nor does it lack its share of prima donnas.

What do I mean by 'love' in the present context? In conventional language any attempt at a definition will prove elusive and misleading. Freud cut the Gordian knot by showing that we, in fact, communicate from one unconscious to another. Provided, then, that we function openly and spontaneously without resorting to strategies and a need to hide by impersonating a role of some professional concoction; that we are able to respond warmly if – hopefully – offered a hug; that we can intuit when a personal aside is pleaded for, then we provide the catalyst without which treatments may go on for ever and even then leave scars that need not have remained. I regret bitterly that it took me so long to arrive at this unshakeable conviction.

As in all our human relationships, the important thing is to know our authentic place at the wheel of ameliorating human suffering and ineptitude. An artificial, second-hand approach will always be picked up as such and prove distancing and counter-productive. Nor should anything I may say be taken as blaming parents. They too were children once and suffer grief enough in some secret knowledge of their failure.

To say anything in general about sexual abuse must be left to those who specialise in working with these patients. My own clinical encounters are limited so that anything I have to say springs from a small number of cases rather than from textbook information.

There is, of necessity, a large body of human experience that we all have in common. Sexual abuse is happily not part of this common experience, so we learn as we go along. In the course of my training, I underwent – the only word I can find for it – the barest minimum of supervision. I wanted to approach each individual patient as if I only 'knew' that which had become a part of me in the course of my own analysis and what I had mopped up instinctively in the course of reading, reflection and dreams. In other words, I am not an authority on anything other than personal experience. While this may raise eyebrows at such arrogance, it seems safer to me to proceed in that manner.

When I felt at sea in my work with a certain patient I brought these quandaries to the five-times-a-week sessions of my own analysis. There I was helped to understand how that which puzzled or even tormented me occupied a hiding place at the heart of my personal difficulties. But however painful the background from which these stemmed, it fortunately did not include sexual abuse.

I can remember a single occasion where I watched my father urinate. This brief glimpse of one function of the penis has remained with me all my life as something uncanny and potentially frightening. My family being what it was, it could certainly not be talked about.

This encounter was, of course, not with the erect penis. One patient of mine, then in her late thirties, had never seen the organ in its flaccid condition until she was in her twenties and one day when she was travelling on the Underground a man sitting opposite exposed himself. She could not believe her eyes. As he opened his trousers there emerged something tiny and pink. She sat there hypnotised, wondering what it was. She had never, as a child, been allowed to see her younger brothers naked.

As a child, and very young woman, her sexual encounters had all been within the wider category of rape. Men in the world at large somehow sussed out her vulnerability – an inability to protect herself, to say 'no', as she had been unable to say no to her abusing father. They would masturbate, even ejaculate against her unprotesting body on the crowded Underground so that she had to find the 'ladies' to wash herself. On her part, submission belonged to the realm of repetition compulsion that plays such an ominous part with these patients. She dealt with these situations, as she had dealt with her father's 'sexual games', by a process of dissociation, of leaving her body and floating up to the ceiling from where she observed the incest scene below as if it did not concern her.

As I sat and listened to her, often in great pain, I could only struggle to put myself in her place in such unspeakable scenarios, feeling almost guilty that I had escaped what I can only describe as such atrocities.

In my own practice I have encountered two categories of women who have suffered incest. First, there are those like Sister Mary, who at the initial interview can somehow convey that they are seeking help for paralysing memories of violation. Second, there are the others who have very little, if anything, to say for themselves. Body language speaks for them. From the outset they present as perceptibly terrified. They panic, gather up their belongings, and seem about to flee from the room. They are quite unable to use the couch. I will always remember how one such patient, sitting – I should say crouching – in her chair, almost vomited on an occasion when – not aware that I wanted to comfort her – I stroked the pillow on the empty couch. This, it occurred to me, she saw as a preamble to my evil intentions. One day she arrived with a crippling headache. In this pattern we came to recognise that these headaches served to stop her thinking about a pain other than that in her head. Psychic pain only surfaced in the slowest of stages. None of these phenomena she as much as commented on, and initially my attempts at interpretations met with total panic and inability to breathe: the soma in total disarray.

In time, dreams began to repeat an identical story. Dreams of a little girl who plunged into water where she almost drowned, presumably back to mummy's inside as a sanctuary.[10] There were variations on the theme of being chased by men. One was enormously large and dressed in purple mohair, the engorged penis in its nest of pubic hair. She was chased by a man with a rounders bat who said, 'run, run, I can't help myself'. She runs into bushes, comes out crying without her stockings and weeping, 'no one helps'. A girl is impaled on a rounders bat.

But, however vivid these recurring dreams were, actual memories were painfully slow to emerge; and, for a long time, the patient feared that she was telling lies, inventing even her dreams to gain attention.

There has recently been publicity, particularly from across the Atlantic, concerning therapists who break up whole families by instilling false memories of incest into their patients. In the absence of memories one clearly has to tread very carefully, but body language and, above all, dreams are hard to invent with careful scrutiny over a period of time.

---

[10] Water was also connected with suicide: jumping off bridges across the River Thames.

Conspicuous also is the total inability to trust any other human being, let alone the therapist. In the transference with this patient, I would endlessly become the abusing father. Once she was able to find words for her states of frozen terror she feared that I was in cahoots with the West family[11] and that there were corpses under my floorboards. To leave the room she had to pass my chair, terrified that I would leap up and assault her.[12] She experienced her existence as being thrust for life between a rock of abandonment and a hard place of being at the mercy of her father.

Since the unconscious has no cognisance of time, violation from the past was constantly projected into the future so that she could experience no joy and envisage no carefree future, as it did simply not exist.

In the case of Sister Mary, whose memories were partly intact, even if initially split from affect so that I had to hold her feelings for her until painting put her in touch with them, the journey to recovery was considerably facilitated by painting. (This did not appeal to the other patients.) Even if, as she tells us, she spent the first few months ensconced in the protective armour of her black coat, she was, within the relatively short time span of a few months, able to unbutton, then to remove it. A healthy part of her personality had, seemingly, survived intact. Once she was able to paint 'the devil man', to get in touch with her pent-up feelings of murderous hate, and this was no longer projected into me, she could, little by little, begin to trust me. We were also building on a good-enough start in life, which my other patients lacked.

It strikes me as difficult to conceive of incest becoming an established pattern, as it was in the case of Sister Mary, where a child has a close, loving and trusting relationship with a good-enough mother. On the other hand, we are in a country where nothing can be ruled in or out. We know that 'The theatre of the mind' can be more inventive than anything we are likely to view on the stage.[13]

Where memories are initially lacking, much of their mental hinterland will surface as the body speaking in 'conversation symptoms' with dire urgency. Hopefully, gynaecologists and others are becoming aware of the historicity of certain symptoms that on the

---

[11] Fred and Rosemary West, from Gloucestershire, who abused and murdered numbers of young women in their home and then buried the bodies around the premises.

[12] At the time I used to remain seated in the chair when a patient left, as I had fractured my femur.

[13] Joyce McDougall (1986). 'Theatres of the Mind'. Illusion and Truth on the Psychoanalytic Stage. Free Association Books, London.

surface appear to call for instant intervention, drastic surgery – even hysterectomies. Nor can major dental procedures, since the mouth is a symbol for the vagina, be ruled out as belonging to that domain.

All patients will suffer considerable self-disgust. This is projected into their appearance. One patient I have in mind, beautiful by any standards, was convinced that she was ugly; that she was dirty and would never be clean. These convictions she projected into me convinced that I found her repulsive, in other words that I surely shared in her own denigration of her fine looks, her intelligence and her courage in wrestling with so much terror. There were times when she, too, was suicidal.

But we should not forget that, on the other hand, there are women who have suffered incest yet might appear to live a good-enough marriage and become mothers of a family. It is, perhaps, one attempt to repair in their children the damage that was inflicted on themselves. My patient above, for all her wish at times to die, became the mother of several children, although, inevitably, a bad choice of husband ultimately left her as a single parent. She needed to prove to herself that she did not have to pass on the deplorable experience. She feared in retrospect that she had been too busy being the perfect mother. Could this have damaged her children? They all seemed to be thriving in early adult life, which she found hard to believe. She only broke down after they had all left home.

Lastly, is there anything to be said about the phenomenon of the silent patient, the one who day by day and week by week continues to come to her sessions and yet remains unable to speak while her silence communicates the unspeakable; is there anything more to say than about the taboo on speaking, imposed by the internalised abusing father?

If we return to these individuals' dysfunctional families – the culture that they came from, we find one thing in common, which is a striking poverty of language of the emotions. Now, to some extent, this is nothing unusual. A dialogue today often consists largely of 'you know what I mean'. But that still conveys a search for meaning whereas what I am referring to here is an absence of, indeed a prohibition on, the vocabulary of a facility for containment, of words that convey neediness and distress, words that a good-enough mother would usually respond to, interpret and contain: words such as 'scared', 'leave me alone', 'I hate you', 'I want out', 'it hurts'. But the same brick-wall attitude belongs to words of affection: 'missing', 'wanting'. And sobs and tears are prohibited as signs of weakness, of being a nuisance, a disgrace.

This stultifying pattern has been described as 'a defence against affective vitality'; a condition of 'blocked affect'. Analysts who have devoted themselves to researching the condition have given it the name of Alexithymia, from 'Greek, a: "without", lexis: "word", thumos: "heart" or "affectivity", in other words, "having no words for emotion".'[14]

Before effective psychotherapy with such patients can begin they need to learn a whole new vocabulary. Here the therapist has, initially, to be the mother who knows and is not afraid of words such as 'panic', 'difficulties', 'fear of dying' or 'doing away with oneself' (that these are not 'wicked'); above all 'hate' (seen as 'evil') and much more. Until this is understood and can begin to be remedied, the silent patient may appear merely stubborn since she can only present the psychotherapist with infinite unspoken anguish, with the sense of being lost in some no man's land from which there is no way out. After all, where words are missing, or only uttered under threat of parental disapproval, this is how the victim feels.

Where Sister Mary was concerned, we saw that she already possessed a certain limited vocabulary, even if most of it was split off from feeling. She had, after all, worked with children who had suffered all manner of neglect and abuse, emotional and physical. It was only, as we will see, when she encountered little girls who had been sexually abused by their father, that her maternal capacity failed her and she broke down.

Much patience and, yes, love will be required to extricate the incest victim from her frozen isolation, her self-hatred and despair; but the rewards, as we shall see, are also almost unspeakable. But here, in a wealth of the language of thanksgiving and celebration, Sister Mary shares with us her own reward in her deeply touching style of telling, while my own rests between the lines.

---

[14] 'Theatres of the Mind', p.159.

PART ONE

A tribute to Freud

My love affair with Freud began not with his collected works, nor the Jones biography, but later, with a little book[1] I stumbled on by pure chance. Indeed, it was not to be found on any shelf of our textbooks, the reading list of training years, and must have been out of print for many years at a time.

In the foreword by Norman Holmes Pearson we are already intrigued, seduced; sensing a treat to come: 'I envy everyone who has not yet read it'. Nor, as I would discover, had colleagues, who were widely read, shared my discovery.

This should come as no surprise. The Freud we delight to meet in the company of this enchanting author, if ever one set pen to paper, might well be slated in our day for his disregard of boundaries, the spontaneity with which 'the Professor' carried on.

The book sets the scene. It is 1938, weeks before the fatal *Anschluss*, as the assault of Hitler's army on neighbouring Austria was euphemistically called. H.D., at 47 years of age, is the great magician's junior by exactly 30 years. She brings her own reputation as poet and author, a golden child in her time.[2] And so we should not be surprised to find her analysis with Freud preceded by a delightful correspondence.

The master apologises that he has had to keep her waiting a little longer for a place. He writes again that it may be as well, owing to the 'biting' cold; an epidemic of Grippe (flu). Would she not rather come at the beginning of spring – perhaps in April or in May? In the event, the first series of H.D.'s sessions with Freud began in March of that year to run for something like four months. The sessions certainly extended into summer, when Freud continued to see his

---

[1] H.D. (1985). *Tribute to Freud*, revised edition. Carcanet Press, Manchester.
[2] Recently acclaimed as one of the finest poets of her era, H.D. was Hilda Doolitte.

patients in his summer residence at Döbling. H.D. saw him five times a week, to return for five further weeks towards the end of the following year.

Once he knew her favourite hour, Freud arranged H.D.'s time for the late afternoon.

> **'You would have liked such special treatment: treatment for a princess.' I hear the voice of 'my' analyst comment, with a hint of irony.**
> **'Certainly,' I reply.**
> **But this is 1993 when I return once a week after a break of several years, and ten years of the full routine.**

Well on into the book the poet's reminiscing of her initiation into the famous sanctuary gives a magical taste of the ageing mentor, as it also does of the woman and her style. A lover of antiquities, she had been wholly unprepared for Freud's collection of bibelots. These riveted her entire attention until he protested, 'and, I thought, a little sadly, said: "You are the only person who has ever come into this room and looked at the things in the room before looking at me".'

But worse was to come:

> **A little lion-like creature came padding towards me – a lioness, as it happened. She had emerged from the inner sanctum or manifested from under or behind the couch; anyhow, she continued her course across the carpet. Embarrassed, shy, overwhelmed, I bend down to greet this creature. But the Professor says, 'Do not touch her – she snaps – she is very difficult with strangers.' Strangers? Is the Soul crossing the threshold a stranger to the door-keeper? It appears so. But, though no accredited dog-lover, I like dogs and they oddly and sometimes unexpectedly 'take' to me. If this is an exception I am ready to take the risk. Unintimidated but distressed by the Professor's somewhat forbidding manner, I not only continue my gesture towards the little chow, but crouch on the floor so that she can snap better if she wants to. Yofi is her name. Yofi snuggles her nose into my hand and nuzzles her head in delicate sympathy, against my shoulder ...**

Our objective is not to analyse the poet – one-time fiancée of Ezra Pound, former wife of Richard Aldington, lover of D.H. Lawrence (who was, according to her biographer, the one great love of her life[3]) and friend to Havelock Ellis and others of her time. Clearly, she had

---

[3] Janice S. Robinson (1982). *H.D., The Life and Work of an American Poet.* Houghton Mifflin: Boston.

suffered significant inner turmoil, even breakdown at times. She had
lost her brother at the front during the war; her first child had been
stillborn; she had been betrayed by Aldington and, most alarming
perhaps, there had been two occasions, during a stay in Greece, of
dream-like hallucinations – times when reality and dream fused in
episodes of terror.

The hallucinations were, she relates, her only symptom that
Freud took seriously. He suggested that she had travelled to Helas to
be united with her late mother, whose name was Helen. Be that as it
may: '... of course, there is always something more to be found out',
Freud added. How vividly, how life-size, Freud the genius emerges
from this warp and weft of words. The tremendous passion of the
man, 77 at the time, and stricken with advancing cancer, suffering
from pain and with a prosthesis inserted in his upper jaw.

Unforgettable are the septuagenarian's outbursts:

> I did not know what enraged him suddenly. I veered round off the
> couch, my feet on the floor. I do not know exactly what I had said ... I
> do not want to become involved in the strictly historical sequence. I
> wish to recall the impressions, or rather I wish the impressions to
> recall me ... The Professor himself is uncanonical enough; he is beat-
> ing with his hand, with his fist, on the head-piece of the old-fashioned
> horsehair sofa that had heard more secrets than the confession box
> of any popular Roman Catholic father-confessor in his heyday.

This happens on several occasions. We gather that this grandfather,
head of his family, founder of access to the human mind, is occasion-
ally full of sound and fury. We have been warned what to expect:
'The professor said, "The trouble is – I am an old man – you do not
think it worth your while to love me".' Have we not already heard his
dismay that on entering the famous consulting room, before H.D.
looked at him she had made, without a second thought, straight for
his antiquities?

It is, of course, still early spring. Lying on the leather couch H.D.
reached for a little rug. Despite the old-fashioned tiled stove, it seems
that she felt the cold. The professor secured a thicker rug, one of real
fur, for her. It is a tale of a thousand-and-one nights, or rather late
afternoons. H.D. felt afraid. She mentions that her father never hit her,
whereas Freud's arm would sometimes shoot out from his armchair
behind her, as his words might erupt when she offended him.

There is also the confiding Freud, the grieving father who lost his
favourite daughter. When H.D.'s associations once turned to the last
year of the war, Freud 'had reason to remember the epidemic of

Grippe which had carried Sophie away. "She is here", he said, and he showed me a tiny locket that he wore, fastened to his watch-chain.'

Had he found her again in this analysand? Is it this that could account for the old man's intimacy? Is it just that he is old? Or did he habitually oppose any 'mechanisation of the technique' in this manner?

He divulged to H.D. something, here and there, of the mysterious Dutchman whose hour preceded her own: an attractive man of many parts. Flying his own plane back from Africa, 'the flying Dutchman' was killed. It was her devastation at his death that brought H.D. back to the Bergasse for a few more sessions in the following year. 'You have come to replace him,' Freud suggested. He revealed to this analysand how he feared for the future of his grand-children and instructed her: 'Please, never, I mean at any time, in any circumstance, endeavour to defend me, if and when you hear abusive remarks made about me and my work.'

On another occasion, when H.D. spoke of 'ambivalence', uncer-tain how to pronounce the word, she asked where the accent ought to fall. The reply came: 'Do you know, I myself have always wondered. I often wish that I could find someone to explain these matters to me.' It is surprising to read that Freud spoke English with-out a perceptible trace of accent; that he would, in the middle of a session, take up one of the figures on his desk and expound on it in the context of their exchange. But at other times: 'he will sit there quietly, like an old owl in a tree! He will shoot out an arm, sometimes somewhat alarmingly, to stress a point ... or say, "Ah – now – we must celebrate THIS ... Today we have tunnelled very deep". Of his work he explained, "I struck oil. It was I who struck oil. But the contents of the oil wells have only just been sampled. There is oil enough, mate-rial enough for research and exploitation, to last fifty years, to last one hundred years – or longer."'

In 1936, days after Freud's 80th birthday:

All your white cattle safely arrived ...' I had imagined I had become insensitive to praise or blame. Reading your kind lines and getting aware of how I enjoyed them I first thought I had been mistaken about my firmness. Yet on second thoughts I concluded I was not. What you gave me, was not praise, was affection and I need not be ashamed of my satisfaction.
Life at my age is not easy, but spring is beautiful and so is love, Yours affectionately, Freud.

' A gift of gardenias – Freud's favourite flower.

H.D. was to go in search of gardenias on a final occasion. It was late in 1938. She found some in a West End florist and sent them to Freud's new home in London,[5] with a card: 'To greet the return of the Gods'. 'Affectionately yours, Sigm. Freud' came back the reply.

She saw him for the last time in the summer of 1939 – a conventional gathering only weeks before his death and the outbreak of war. Others present were seated, near him, in a solemn circle, as if already at a wake. Freud was 83 years old.

For many years have I longed to share these reminiscences. Have I been carried away by her intoxicating writing, that of a poet weaving a spell? Or by the privilege of meeting Freud behind the scenes, an encounter steeped in intimacy? I remember an occasion, an evening at the Freud Museum for the launch of a book. It had been my first visit. I was told that I was free to enter his consulting room, to spend some time in there alone – a phenomenal trust. As I stood beside the desk, in sole occupation, a dream transformed into reality, I simply burst into tears. It was entirely too much. I belonged to the chosen few. It was hard to believe as I pinched myself that, no, I was not dreaming. And H.D.'s book had a similar effect. Where Sister Mary is concerned it proved an enduring influence, a memorable initiation.

Freud none the less confined himself to a *verbal* exchange. There is no hint that management pertaining to a medical model queered the pitch of the proceedings, as in the account that follows, where we now encounter Winnicott from the pen of Doctor Margaret Little.[6]

---

[5] 20 Maresfield Gardens, London NW3. Now the Freud Museum.
[6] Little M (1985).*Psychotic Anxieties and Containment. A Personal Record of an Analysis with Winnicott.* Jason Aronson Inc, Northdale, New Jersey & London.

An approach to Winnicott

Margaret Little, a psychoanalyst herself, turned to Winnicott after an impasse occurred during her training analysis, leaving her painfully aware that the core of her illness remained totally untouched. According to her own account her rigid training analyst had simply failed to recognise the nature of her difficulties.

Little reminds us that, by 1913, Freud had discovered that psychoanalysis, initially concerned with later oedipal issues, could prove ineffective once a growing number of people were seeking help with 'far less tractable, psychotic types of anxiety', and that numbers of practitioners marked time in a rearguard action.

Analysing small children in their play with toys, Mrs Klein had focused on stages of development earlier than those Freud had brought to light. Her findings introduced new concepts and a new clinical approach within the Freudian ethos.

Although he warmly acknowledged certain areas of Klein's work, Winnicott evolved a very personal approach rooted in his long experience as clinical director of a children's hospital.[1] He was firm in his belief that there is no such thing as a baby, only a mother-and-baby unit as a total environment. Where this containment suffers a failure to bond on a premature dissolution of the symbiotic bond, he saw the outcome in terms of: 'environmental deficiency disease'. This gives rise to a 'false self' in a desperate strategy to cover inner emptiness, and to psychotic-type anxieties of imminent annihilation – early life cast adrift.

To approach this disaster, Winnicott saw a need for 'total active adaptation' on the part of the analyst. This, in his view, demanded areas of management that could foster a return to the roots of early failure reserved for those who needed it. He termed it 'regression to

---

[1] Paddington Green Children's Hospital.

dependence'. As far as Little was concerned, '... the approach of Winnicott showed a more human face of psychoanalysis than that seen before.' It inevitably brought anxiety and controversy, as well as some warm support.

Here we need to understand that whereas Winnicott attributed the more severe types of illness to an early breakdown in the maternal environment, Klein, and later Bion, placed the crux of the matter in the infant's constitution, in an inability to learn to deal with frustration. In other words, here is an infant who, from the word go, annihilates his own potential and cannibalises the early psyche. This catastrophe of the past is projected into the future in expectation of doom and imminent annihilation.

It would seem probable that both ideologies share a bedrock of truth. Certainly Little found what she was looking for in Winnicott's care, and experience will show that where analysis fails a patient in one or the other camp, subsequent help may be found by crossing to the other. Certainly residual warfare must be counterproductive where we need to understand something more of the factors that might determine a choice.

According to her own account, Little felt she had been helped in her very first session:

> **I lay curled up tight, completely hidden under the blanket, unable to move or speak. Winnicott was silent throughout the session and only at the end did he say, 'I don't know, but I have the feeling that you are shutting me out for some reason.'**

It came to her with enormous relief that he 'could admit to not knowing', rather than browbeating her into submission to concepts that had no place in this phase of her treatment. Clearly, Winnicott was already on the track of a psychotic or delusional transference – an infant in terror of a confused, intrusive early mother, ruling the patient's inner world. Indeed, he would later say: 'your mother is unpredictable, chaotic and she organises chaos around her'.

Little, for her part, saw such interventions – anathema to other schools – 'like a revelation. It made it possible for me to understand much of what I already knew ...' Certainly, in my own experience, patients value confirmation until they trust their own perceptions.

Little writes, with evident relief, of Winnicott's emphasis on 'holding' all aspects of and around the patient and how, she relates, this extended literally to his holding her two hands clasped between his own, while she lay beneath the blanket he provided: 'silent, inert, withdrawn, in panic, rage and tears, asleep or sometimes dreaming'.

Since she tended to leave these sessions in a self-destructive frame of mind, Winnicott would take her car keys and have her lie in a quiet room until he saw fit to return them. Each session ended with coffee and biscuits. In other words, management played a part in the proceedings from the start.

The degree of regression that such primal care fostered was seen by Little (as by others) as 'regression to dependence for life itself – to the level of infancy, and sometimes even to pre-natal life'. It involved her therapist 'entering into and sharing an experience in such a way that emotion that had to be dammed-up could be set free'.

Accordingly, in her account, we slowly gravitate towards her deeply moving experience of Winnicott's management of 'regression to dependence'. This, it seems, he instituted as he became aware that a particular patient had, at an unconscious level, still remained undecided as to whether he or she existed: whether to live or to die.

Around the fifth summer break of her analysis, he obtained her agreement that she be hospitalised as a consenting patient in an asylum setting that respected his approach. He took her there by train himself, and later fetched her home again.

Little describes how:

> The hospital care was total and interference minimal; everything was provided and no demand made. I spent the time sleeping, reading, writing, and painting, sometimes on the walls of my room; playing, in fact. I wandered in the garden and roamed the streets; when it rained a ward orderly would fetch me in with umbrella and waterproof. When my feet were blistered the sister dressed them and told me, 'You should have telephoned for a car to fetch you.'
> There might be distress or disturbance going on round me but the place went on BEING, and holding and looking after me, calm and apparently unperturbed.

In other words, the setting provided a 'good-enough' early mother as a first experience of such a possibility.

For those who claim that such regression therapy leads to more of the same behaviour, Little informs us that within a few weeks she was back at work, and her own analysis now entered its termination stage. It is worth pausing here for a moment to quote from her moving summing-up of the person she was after her analysis – a question that is often asked:

> I was no longer a non-person, my identity being acknowledged by D.W. and other people; I was established as a training analyst ... I could Be and Do, asserting myself without undue guilt or anxiety or

paranoid reaction ... I was 'not recognizable for the same person'.

I have gone on since then in self-analysis ... reconsidering the value of the regression, seeing it more clearly, especially the time in hospital as a challenge to determine which would prove stronger, the sickness or the health, which were both there.

I have had success and failure, pleasure and pain, in both my professional and personal life and have found life worth living as it had scarcely been before ... For me, ambivalence and anxiety of course remain, for no analysis ever does away with them or is ever complete.

The overriding feeling is one of deep and lasting gratitude, for D.W. enabled me to find and free my 'true self', my spontaneity, creativeness, and ability to play; he restored my sanity without leaving me 'only sane'. I am in touch with the child in me who wants to play ... to use what she has been given ... while my more mature self is endeavouring to express the true thanks I feel by giving this account of his work with me. ('I don't know whether I like it, but it's what I meant', as Vaughan Williams said of his Fourth Symphony.)

I hope I have managed here to prepare the ground for the tale of Sister Mary who, like Little, would discover her own true self, her 'open road'.

PART TWO
Sister Mary
tells her story

Chapter One

'Doctor Fernandes', the message said, 'would prefer to see me in the surgery rather than visit me at home in the convent' because her scheduled rounds to our nursing home put limits on her available time. Besides, she added, her surgery would provide more privacy and secure the confidentiality required for the nature of my visit.

This kindly doctor, who only weeks after my return to London had treated me for a damaged Achilles tendon, had about her a warmth and wisdom reminiscent of the 'flower lady' of my childhood. I was instantly drawn to her, vaguely sensing, yet half-fearful, that she might have answers or maybe even reasons for all the pain and hurt in every part of my body or in my mind – I was not in the least bit sure.

The surgery waiting room was still full when I arrived a little after noon, nearly six years ago. A single chair stood empty in the far corner of the room and I went to it, determined to ignore the rising panic, lest I took flight and ran. I leafed with unseeing eyes, repeatedly, cover to cover, through a book. When the receptionist called my name, I walked unsteadily down the small hallway to room four.

As the door closed behind me, blocking out the sights and sounds of the waiting room, Dr Fernandes addressed my unspoken anxiety saying:

'It's all right, you are my last patient today, so just tell me what you can in your own time. I hear you have been through a pretty tough time.'

When I had finally finished, after using an endless amount of her tissues, she said:

'I really feel you should have some professional help. There are some wonderful people living in the area whom I could recommend; one a religious sister, the other a lady, a psychotherapist. I can refer you if you would like me to ...'

I said I thought I might like to go to the lady psychotherapist.

'I think you might like her, she's had her own troubles and knows what it is to suffer.'

'But it isn't as simple as all that,' I protested. I would have to get permission from our Mother General, who at the time was at the other side of the world. I said that I was not at all sure that I would be allowed to have psychotherapy.

'I know your Mother General,' she said. 'I think you will find there won't be a problem'.

And with those words ringing in my ears I left the surgery tearful but strangely comforted, feeling far less alone. It seemed as though I had come into a warm, cosy house on a cold winter's day. The task I had been given to do seemed small: to go home and think seriously about psychotherapy and discuss it with my superiors. The prospect of this hung in the air with all the threatening danger of gathering thunder-clouds, yet I chose to ignore unpleasant thoughts because, hand in hand, for now at least, I felt an enormous sense of relief as I walked up the street, which was now roaring with rush-hour traffic, back to the convent.

Mother General's return was only days away when Dr Fernandes brought the news that the psychotherapist was prepared to see me. There was a telephone number where she could be reached for an appointment. Like bubbles bursting in the air, the relief and comfort simply evaporated leaving in their wake the heartburn of emptiness I so dreaded. For days I stormed at my friend, Sister Jan, that no one would or could ever understand: not a therapist and most certainly not a Mother General, who was so good and holy and clean. How could I tell her the things that had happened to me?

She would have to send me away for ever from the congregation and nobody would have anything to do with me ever again. What, then, would happen to me? I would go on just as I had always done, I suppose. I had survived so far and could again, once I got myself together.

But Jan's solid attention to those most in need of care won that day and many more battles yet to come. Finally, we agreed she would prepare the way for me with the Mother General; support me with her friendship through the course of psychotherapy and even come with me to the appointments when the time came.

Mother General's compassion for my plight, when we finally met, touched the depths of a very sore heart; soothed the raw, jagged edges of all the hurt and brought some relief. Her care and concern stayed with me through all those times during the following four years when it seemed as though there would be no end to the pain and hurt of sadness. When I worried endlessly about fees and expense, her reply was always the same: 'Money is money; it can be replaced. We cannot replace one of our sisters.'

Anything that could be done to help me to heal would be done. This mother epitomised the mother of my dreams. It all seemed like a miracle, yet I should have known it would be so. Had I not lived with these sisters for almost a quarter of a century at the time and, furthermore, experienced the congregation's maternal attitude towards its members more than once? Why, then, was I so surprised now? In my precarious state of mind I had failed to recognise all the previous goodness, kindness and warmth willingly given to me during those years.

Dr H. was expecting the call when Jan phoned for an appointment. I marked off the intervening days until the assigned date with roller-coaster feelings of doomsday, hardly daring to breathe lest I woke to find it had all been a dream.

It was a wet December afternoon, just before Christmas, when my friend and I set off for my first appointment with Dr H. An icy wind chilled me still more as I walked down the road towards the house feeling very alone; fearful of everything that moved and most especially the children we passed. Even my friend at my side did nothing to minimise the terror I found so hard to keep in check. It seemed as if I was going to hospital for surgery. I became increasingly frightened as we neared the house and my companion remarked: 'This area doesn't seem very nice or safe', giving voice to my unspoken thoughts. 'Now, remember,' she said, before going down the steps to the red door, 'you must not tell her about the suicidal thoughts, otherwise she might not take you.'

Instantly my mind seemed to hold a sort of banner before me with the words: 'She will understand: she's had her own troubles.'

The key at the end of the cord with which I was to let myself in as the lady had explained, threaded easily through the letterbox. This made me feel more than a little perplexed: maybe Jan was right; perhaps it was not a very safe place, almost anyone could freely get in and listen.

The door opened into a narrow hallway with two chairs, a table and bookshelves stacked with books. I just wanted to curl up in the corner and read. Another door opened with the sound of wood on carpet and a regally tall lady appeared. With a smile just reaching her eyes, she came forward and introduced herself. My mind flew away as she and my friend exchanged some words about heating and the need for a fire to keep warm on so cold a day and how it was a little unusual to have a patient accompanied to appointments, even more so to have the escort wait during sessions.

All this I know I heard but with an ever-growing fear that she might not take me; perhaps even think I was too dangerous; I just stood there waiting for someone to shout at me. Instead, turning, she said: 'Do come in.' She pointed the way through two doors, set either side of the door jambs, and into a room with a window that looked up on to the pavement just beyond a tiny patch of garden. This room felt safe. There were books and plants; lamps and pictures on the walls; a long, narrow couch and a mustard-yellow settee, on which I sat – although I would have liked to wrap myself up in the colourful blankets on the couch or even sit on the window-seat beside the plants.

On that day and for very many sessions following, I declined the invitation to remove my black, buttoned and belted raincoat and sat on the far end of the settee, hands deep in my pockets, petrified that I might say something wrong and be sent away. I might even let something slip about just how terrible and hopeless everything seemed: bad enough to think of dying. She might think I was mad too, like they sometimes said of my mother: 'poor Cathleen', they whispered.

I knew I needed my coat for protection, but why, when this lady spoke to me in a soft, gentle voice? She wanted to know why it was I had come to her and what seemed to be the problem. She was quietly awaiting a reply. I heard a voice that certainly seemed to be mine say: 'Dr Fernandes thought it was important that I see someone.' 'The question is: what do *you* think,' the lady said.

A tale tumbled out in a torrent of words, barely audible, and a distant, unfamiliar voice told of a recent operation, a hysterectomy; of the experience of freedom and the sense of well-being during the subsequent eight-week convalescent period. It told of how I had dared to believe that this dreamlike peace of mind, which had escaped me for so long, might finally stay with me; until one day the 'heartburn' feeling returned and with it the terrible memories of abuse. It told of a sense of despair that made my waking hours more reminiscent of a balancing act on a taut high-wire, without a pole for support or a safety net, which, in turn, triggered a raging anger which I felt I could no longer contain.

I told her how the anger had spilled out in a wretched letter to my father, vowing never to see him again. I told her of the way in which I had broken the news of all this to my youngest sister, K., on the telephone and out of the blue, long before she and I were ready to handle the after-shock and fall-out it would cause within the family. I tried to explain the fragmentation: how we had all fallen apart; it was all my fault, putting brothers and sisters on both sides of separate fences, for ever it seemed.

Finally, the lady wanted to know a little about my friends and family: the house in which I had lived and my school days and even at what stage I had made the break with home and what had influenced me to enter the convent. Hardly had all this information been given, when it seemed she was somehow satisfied that I was not too dangerous, for she said we would meet once a week. She set out the terms and fees and asked if I had a preference for a time or day.

'Thursdays, in the afternoon, would be best for me,' I said. 'I would be off duty and nobody need then know where I was.'

We set the date for after Christmas: Thursday in the second week of January 1991. She rose quietly, opened each door with a good-bye and I was out in the small hallway again. My friend was still there, with instant questions and concern: 'How did you get on? What was it like? Are you coming back again?'

I could not answer. Outside the room I had just left, the world seemed to me a more dangerous place than I had ever previously known but I could not quite understand why; on another level, it seemed like prize-giving day and the honours had been awarded to me.

Jan was still putting her knitting in her bag halfway down the street. I could not tell her of the treatment my petrified thoughts had just received. I was certain in my mind that we had been to a funeral service where my thoughts had been buried in a very shallow grave just beneath the surface of the ground. I went home to await the next appointment in the new term, after the Christmas break, when, the lady had promised, 'the real work would begin'.

Early in the new year I was back again at the red door. The key, to my amazement, was still hanging on the end of its cord and seemed to bid me welcome, giving rise to a sort of heady jubilance, streaked through with shades of panic, for, as I tried to open the door, the key resisted and had to be forced slightly. But the lady seemed pleased to see me when she appeared. Her smile suggested that she might even allow me to stay. 'Let me show you where the toilet is before we begin.'

And then she stood slightly aside to let me go before her into the room where the sight of wonderfully coloured blankets brought Africa instantly to mind with its sunny blue skies, laughing children and happier days. Tears pricked my eyes and I sat on the mustard-coloured settee feeling full of a deep sorrow and wishing to recapture something of that carefree time.

Barely was I seated when, to my horror, the 'Gestapo'[1] materialised before my eyes. They had ways and means of dealing with people like me. Plans were afoot to kill me if I dared talk about anything. Into this stunned and terrorised state of mind, the lady's voice reached me: 'What are you thinking?' she asked.

If I tell her all the thoughts in my mind, I pondered, she might have the 'Gestapo' take me away – just as they had taken my mother each time to a mental hospital. In my experience no one had ever come home from such a place and they certainly never got better. Too dazed with dread to answer, certain that at any moment I would be dragged out of the room, never again to be seen, with no one to check where I was or to care that I was missing, I sat petrified, in total silence. In some compartment of my mind I believed that this lady was on 'their' side – a state of mind that would last many months.

During each successive session I backed further into the corner of the settee, hands clenched tightly into white-knuckled fists deep in my pockets, and replied to the lady only when there seemed no alternative and then barely audibly, so that she said repeatedly: 'Sorry but I can hardly hear you.'

These early days of therapy were painful in the extreme, yet, paradoxically, Thursday could not come soon enough. Once in the room, however, terror wrapped its cold arms about me, enfolding me in an awful silence.

I can vaguely remember hearing the lady stress the importance of saying whatever came into my mind. But how could I? To speak was every bit as dangerous as I had always believed it would be, and most of all when suicidal thoughts were uppermost in my mind!

Yet words did come and I spoke about our house in which five children and two parents lived, each with separate rooms, although in reality the red-brick house we called home was a tiny, three-bedroom house in which seven people lived together, isolated by pain and individual private suffering.

---

[1]'Gestapo' and 'Mafia', are in fact harsh and judgmental parts of a patient's mind that manifest where feelings of unworthiness are very pronounced.

Continuous fear of the unknown bringing fresh disasters plagued my every moment. All too soon the disasters manifested themselves. One afternoon early on in the first term of treatment, the lady said, from what at the time seemed some grand and lofty height, that it would be in my best interests to come alone, without an escort to each session. Nodding agreement, I repeated parrot-like that yes, it would be in my best interests and of course it would give me time to assimilate what happened and came to light during each session: the very essence of the compliant, good girl who wanted to please the *big* people. Silently I screamed back 'how could you, when you neither know nor understand what is in my best interests, and how dare you suggest otherwise'. All she wanted was Jan out of the way! Then she could get rid of me too without fuss or question! But no word of this was verbalised on that day.

It was snowing that afternoon; Kensington Gardens looked like a winter picture postcard as it sparkled silver-white in the late-after-noon sunshine and rang with the laughter of happy children at play: they made a spectacular landscape of colours: pink and green, lime and yellow, against the snowy scene.

As we walked through the park, I told Jan about the required solo visits, and then trod the lady not once, but twice, into the ground and trampled her underfoot in sheer rage, while Jan, aghast at the outburst, looked on in amazement. We had to go home immediately. I could not stand another second in the park. It seemed that the day was ruined and I had managed to spoil even the children's fun, although their happy, laughing voices still reached our ears right out in the street.

From that time onwards I drove myself the three minutes it took by car to reach the red door, only rarely walking when there was no other possible means of getting there. Local children were almost always on the street, and I could hardly bear to pass them. Their deprived appearance evoked memories I was as yet ill-equipped to face and, besides, the ever-present 'Gestapo' was deterrent enough and remained powerfully in control so that the secret truth of my story lay hidden even if I did have a strong sense that the lady would stay and listen to me.

One day I felt compelled to ask, with some trepidation, how long the course was likely to take and although the reply satisfied me, what I saw as evasiveness filled me with longing and horror. It did not enter my head that our particular journey was to last three full years and some four months.

Chapter Two

For many months to come a barrier, strong and wide as the ancient walls of my home town and equally high, stood between the lady and me. Occasional chinks of light seeped through the fortress shedding brightness on my senses and I could even hear the lady without difficulty say: 'What are you thinking?', always in a kindly tone.

I would emerge from a distance, long enough to tell some more of a little girl's pain. Words were such dangerous things. Look at what had happened to my mother. Nobody had listened to her and they said she was mad. I would sit in total silence throughout almost the entire session. The 'don't you dare talk, don't say a word' key locking in the hopeless heartburn.

Then, one day, to my profound shock, the lady said that since we had made little or no progress and seemed only to waste a great deal of time, we would give ourselves a few more weeks 'to see how things went' and then make a decision as to whether or not to continue.

With that whiff of very real and imminent danger filling the air, I came to life, or rather the little girl who had suffered such deprivation sprang out of limbo and into action. 'Lose this lady after waiting so very many years? Never,' the child-me seemed to exclaim.

In my mind was an image of a little person pulling me up by both hands with such determination but with great difficulty, as children do when they need to show that something simply cannot wait.

'Tell her,' the little voice insisted. 'Please tell her now!'

All the fears of not knowing what to say or how to say it poured out as though from some broken dam. To my indescribable relief the lady picked up everything I had left unsaid: 'Are you afraid you might be mad, as perhaps you felt your mother was?'

Amazed that some of my most secret thoughts had been voiced, that nobody had yet dragged me from the room; and now that my search of the lady's face showed not the slightest displeasure at what I

23

had silently voiced, I whispered that that exactly had been my fear almost all my life. When friends and family noted how alike my mother and I were, it terrified me and the terror in turn paralysed me.

This revelation marked a breakthrough in therapy and although we were still subjected to long silences, they were now of an entirely different type: sometimes spaced out and reflective; and sometimes hostile. Even to the end of the process, the inner 'Gestapo', sometimes joining forces with the 'Mafia', still tried to sabotage the work we did. Although I was petrified by their presence, we continued to work together, for now there seemed to be someone there for me.

If I realised that the 'someone there for me' was the very first seed of trust, replanted after so very many years, that would mature with tender loving care, I did not even tell myself, let alone anyone else. But that seed would take root and continue to grow way beyond the time we agreed to finish our work together.

At that stage neither the lady nor I made mention of such a possibility, for I would have run in panic from such precarious things as trusting anyone; it would only have brought pain, hurt and infinite sadness. I knew this for certain in the depths of my being, and so, as the months went by and the sessions were increased to twice a week, little by little details of my childhood emerged.

While we lived in our grandmother's house things went tolerably well. She was the scaffold supporting my mother and security for us children. When my father was home, however, the sun seemed to shine a brighter shade on the brasses of my grandmother's front door, the tiles in the little hallway gleamed cardinal red and the clock on the stairway chimed in happier tone.

Memories surrounding that house, a place that has remained in my mind as my only *real* home, are vivid with scents, sounds, touch, flowers and colours. Lilac and sweet pea; white lace communion dresses; white crocheted socks and lily of the valley vests. Soft, silky, long-haired 'Captain', our dog; uncle Joe's silver tenor voice raised in song; incense and church candles; sea air and seaweed; warm sandy beaches and Nanna's nightly blessing before we went to sleep after hot chocolate beside her fireplace on cold winter evenings.

When the house on the other side of the square became vacant, it was, we were told, to become our new home; a prospect that seemed to excite the adults infinitely more than it did us children.

'It's not a nice place and we want to stay with Nanna,' we said. But the promise of a bedroom just for the girls that would have pretty wallpaper and a dressing table, kidney-shaped, with a frill and matching window curtains, won our hearts and soon life in that lonely house began.

For a while things went well enough. An ordinary working family; the school year, its holidays, with endless picnics and days out; swimming in the Shannon River, camp fires and sizzling sausages whose aroma drew us like magnets to our mother's side. There, sitting in the shade, wrapped in towels, we ate our meal under a blue sky with soft fluffy clouds. Then, in the evening, just after we were in bed, our father would take up his place on the little landing at the top of the stairway, both our bedroom doors open, and read to us from *Treasure Island*, *Little Women* and *Heidi*. Sometimes he would tell us stories of the far-away places from his Air Force days: Cairo and Tripoli and even Jerusalem. Then back to Long John Silver, *Marooned*, and a grandfather who lived high up in the mountains that were snow-peaked and where children could play, carefree and happy in flower-covered meadows. All this mingled together in my mind with memories of Sunday walks through the nearby fields, where little streams gurgled over mossy rocks and the splashing of children's feet disturbed the tadpoles and the squeals of delight when the tiny creatures could be taken and shown to our father. Then, when it was evening and tea was finished and our mother gone on her weekly visit to one of her sisters, we took our seats around the turf fire and sang songs. Neighbourhood children would come, drawn, like those by the Pied Piper, to take their place wherever there was a space, hanging on to my father's every word, as he told tale after tale of ghosts and the little people.

Those evenings ended with our voices raised in song: 'I love to go a-wandering' and 'The Book that my Mother gave me'; songs that still rekindle in my memory the warmth of those evenings and the love I had for a father who then could do no wrong. A time, indeed, of sheer bliss, compared with what was still to come.

Chapter Three

Winter that year was the coldest in the history of our small city. Snow piled high in our little garden, pipes burst and even our school stayed closed for several days. Was it a foretaste of our ice-age to come?

That summer our youngest sister was born. A beautiful, doll-like little baby, with golden curls and huge brown eyes. But my mother, when they both came from the hospital, seemed so sad. I watched her face, etched with her pain. Sometimes our house was so eerily quiet. When we arrived home from school in the afternoon it seemed there was no one inside although the front door stood open.

An anxious search usually found our mother lying on her bed, the baby beside her, crying. To our dismay and confusion our presence only added to her distress, as if the baby and ourselves were all best forgotten. Henceforth we ceased to exist.

At intervals, life resumed its normal course but became increasingly unpredictable and I soon learned to look and listen and search my mother's face before saying one single word, for now she seemed to be almost always cross and upset, mostly, it seemed, with me. I even felt that she wished me dead.

This was the turning point in all our lives. Our grandmother's help was enlisted but no one could pacify my mother, or bring a smile back to her face; and the aunts and uncles who appeared on our doorstep like malevolent genies, only to disappear and return to their own nice cosy homes, did not do anything to help our predicament. When they had gone, whispered words flew around our heads that poor Cathleen would end up in St Joseph's. Not one of these relatives or visiting 'friends' (with the exception of my grandmother) offered to clean or cook, wash our clothes or offer comfort to the bewildered group that was our family, although their verbal advice was lavishly given and often repeated with its invitation to my poor mother to: 'pull yourself together now and look after the children'. It seemed that she had no ears to hear.

While with a distance of 40 years it is far easier to reflect on this sorry story, at the time I could find neither compassion nor excuse, for to the child I was then it seemed to me that my mother had deserted us when she was most needed. It would take me four decades to find out how much I loved her.

And so began a period that was to have a lasting and traumatic effect on all our lives. Our mother did indeed 'end up in St Joseph's', and so began the first of her admissions, several times a year, into that mental hospital; a place that became a haven and refuge for her; and where her own father had, it transpired, spent half a lifetime.

That his name was never mentioned raised untold anxieties in my mind and his very existence became shrouded in mystery and dread.

Tears prick my eyes even as I write, still very sad, but now able to have compassion for that little Mary, who watched and waited each time for a mother to come home from hospital, elated by the hopeful signs when she seemed to be more like herself and even smile at the first sight of her children.

Yo-yo years followed and a pattern began to emerge within the framework of our existence. Christmas and summer holidays were replaced totally by 'sick and in hospital' and, when they were over, 'Mammy is coming home'. When she was home there was a sense of reprieve and even a measure of safety. Some small semblance of routine was restored. Routine with its predictability was something I longed to have.

In comparison, our all-too-rare visits to our grandparents' house offered such a sanctuary. Routine meal-times, warm, clean sheets, books to read and an aunt who clearly enjoyed and even wanted to spend time in our company. It was she who widened the horizons of our minds, who opened the gates to explore our city,[1] took us on tours to various parts of Ireland and once even to England. She arranged outings to films, concerts and the opera and then tea in a real restaurant. Solace indeed for a lonely child, a waif restored to a sense of belonging, rescued briefly from oblivion.

Thinking back to those years, the love and kindness of this aunt surely kept me just afloat together with care from the 'flower lady'. She was a recent neighbour by marriage, and not once did she turn me from her door but shared her love of flowers willingly, taught me to make crinoline lady dolls and dress them beautifully in pastel blue

---

[1] It was an ancient walled and gated city.

and pink lace. She showed me how to make custard without lumps and bake butterfly cup-cakes in her clean, neat kitchen; so different from the neglect and muddle that ours had become: floor unswept, old food on the table and unwashed dishes everywhere.

Something I cherish to this day, above all, was the invitation to help her to create the prize-winning garden-in-a-plate entry each year for the annual flower festival. In those dark years she fulfilled the role of a loving mother when I believed that I had lost my own, fearing that I must have done something before any grounds for such a fear were rooted in reality. My aunt and the 'flower lady' between them sustained the floundering spirit of a child who might not otherwise have found the courage to survive the worst that was yet to come.

Chapter Four

The 'sick and in hospital' times tell yet another aspect in this drama to add to the existing trauma of absentee parents, who, to all outward appearances, are in fact physically present to some degree.

Where previously my father's normal working day ran from nine to five, Monday to Saturday, delivering bread for one of the city's bakeries, his latest position, gained to his credit through attending night-school courses in sociology, brought fresh hardship. While it provided the means for a more affluent lifestyle, the downside meant that he was more frequently away from home. Conferences, evening appointments and overseas travel consumed even more of his time and energy. While we read of his achievements in the local and even national press, it seemed we had somehow lost him also to this new life. Even when he was in town, come evening and late into the night, our house became a troubled place. As we lay upstairs in our beds, covers pulled up around our ears to block out the sound of the loud music we grew to hate, at full blast throughout our small house, these musical performances became the cause of angry voices raised above the din, until finally and abruptly there was silence and our mother could be heard sobbing.

The following morning brought a strained and ominous silence which we quickly learned to read. Her behaviour further deteriorated in that house-cleaning, no routine of hers in happier days, now started each morning before the sun was up with nerve-racking repetitive singing while she seemed totally oblivious to our presence or even existence. Pots, pans, chairs, the very air was addressed, but no single word was directed at any of the people who were her family. Strangers and neighbours were warmly greeted as long lost friends. Then, just as sure as day follows night, the brewing tension erupted in an almighty row with mother's coat and bag yanked from the stand, and she would rush out of the door in fury. For days no trace or word of her destination would reach us children, nor would anyone offer us a clue except to prophesy her return: 'She'll be back sometime, she's probably staying with one of her friends'. Small comfort indeed, but true enough since after that first occasion she did come back only to disappear again within days, while, standing at the gate or looking from behind lace curtains, we watched her tearfully vanish from our view.

What had we done to make her so ill that only 'treatment' might fix? Were we really so awful? Would we ever see her again and whatever was going to happen to us?

And so our lives ran along two parallel tracks, our mother's condition dictating its entire trend. What her 'condition' might be from one day to the next, from one hour to another, there was no way of knowing. This level of unpredictability with all its light and shade made for a confusion in my mind that would take a virtual lifetime to unravel before I could begin to integrate its unruly substance into a life of my own.

At the time, unable to tell onlookers what was happening, for I had no words, nor would any of those adults really want to know what was destroying our family, we played the 'happy family' game. Five lonely children, two broken parents and a dog continued the charade until it was much too late for a long-overdue intervention.

Had anybody been there to really see our need instead of being frightened away, the disaster that was still to come might possibly have been averted.

How painfully, in those first months of therapy, I recalled the downward spiral of events, the chaotic domestic arrangements of a father desperately trying to hold his family together while he balanced the pressures of his increasingly busy working life with that of being a mother figure with all that the role entails: shopping, cooking and supervising four growing children plus one tiny baby girl. It all seemed to become too much for him and with increasing regularity he was absent from our home until late into the night. Even when it was one of our mother's 'at home' spells it seemed we were all alone in the world where nobody even knew of our existence, for secrecy was paramount. Respectability was all. And to maintain it any price was paid.

Chapter Five

It was at this time the nightly food ritual began. The stairway door was yanked open near midnight.

'Everyone all right up there?' Then, in no time at all, whether it was midnight or two in the morning a 'come and get it' call meant food was the order of the night turned into day. Cabbage and potatoes, mixed with egg and fried, filled our plates when the sleepy band of children appeared around the kitchen table. But there was worse to come.

How it happened that first time is still too painful to recall, mixed with a shame and guilt which sometimes still surfaces and then needs closer attention and further work. Memory tells me that two strong arms lifted me bodily and I was carried down the stairway through the velvet curtain that divided the dining-room/kitchen and swished into place as we passed through the downstairs bedroom door that was our parents' room. Then a father's voice reached my sleepy mind: 'Sleep in here, you're cold'. I snuggled into the mound of blankets until a heavy weight fell on me: I was instantly wide awake, my father's face just above me whispered: 'Hush now, don't make a sound, you'll wake the others upstairs, lie still now. Hold me tight right here', meaning something hard and fat between his legs.

'No, don't move, stay there', and my hand was held fast in place by his own and my panties were pulled off with his other hand. A strange sort of voice whispered over and over above me: 'This is just for us, you and me, no one will ever know.' I was paralysed with terror and something else as well that brought feelings previously unknown. And then a scream began from somewhere deep inside me and a hand covering my mouth wouldn't let the sound out and I gasped and spluttered and could hardly breathe for the pain and terror, certain I was going to die. My face, wet with tears, looked up

33

in horror at this person who was my father, and then my whole body sagged like a rag doll.

The next morning when I awoke curled in a small ball in my own bed in the room I shared with my sister, it seemed it all might have been a nightmare. But father's whistling was back. I heard it as the front door shut, as he got into the car as usual on his way to work. Everything seemed as usual. But nothing would ever be the same or usual again. For when I moved, sore and bruised, and hardly able to stand, when I got out of bed, I knew the nightmare had happened, nothing would ever be as before: the slate of my child-life lay in smithereens.

Afterwards when it seemed I could not bear to be touched, even slightly, by anyone, I was hurt still further by his label, 'Miss Touch-me-not', and when the other children teased and taunted me with this, my father only laughed along with them to my infinite sadness and shame.

But as I limped my way through school that day, heartbroken, orphaned and more abandoned than ever by this latest isolation, I was petrified lest those tears would not stay away while a small sleeve-covered hand brushed them aside, frightened that they would draw questions from our teachers, who were nuns. How would I tell them even while I longed that they might have eyes to see and maybe have a name for all the hurt, pain and sadness there was in every ounce of my body? Yet each time one of them approached, I sank down further in my convent school desk and that day too finally closed on all the trauma and weight. The joy-filled, loving little girl I had once been simply took off and hid until it was safe for her to return at some much later date.

Meanwhile, in my ears, day after day, would echo the sound of the banging of a car door in the night, a door-latch sliding and scraping into place, and loud music, which still has the ability to chill me to the very marrow of my bones to this day, for those sounds open the trap-door on memories buried almost 40 years.

I have memories of feeling worthless, dirty and beyond the pale, an ever-growing certainty that no one, no one on this earth would want to know me again. That all the water and soap could never hope to wash me clean.

Nor was that all. A sense of guilt, of having brought it on myself and not a soul whom I could tell, for then they would banish me to the orphanage down the road where the unwanted children lived, pale-faced and in ugly clothes.

Meanwhile, the hatred of my father, of which I dared not speak to myself for fear it would burst upon the world – that his threats to leave me would come true. Yes, he would not hesitate; he would drive me far away and no one there to take care of me. Did he not threaten constantly? 'Now, remember': how those words burned in me, every hour of the night and day.

Chapter Six

Throughout the following five years the pattern of abuse and deprivation took a firmer hold on all our lives.[1] But a hope stirred in my heart each time my mother returned from hospital and my whole small self echoed my Nanna's greeting: 'Cathleen you're as welcome as the flowers in May.'

Then for a while sunshine and flowers brightened our lives, even if it was sometimes December, but I remained always totally unprepared for the effect my mother's return to the hospital had on me, although long before that day arrived the signs were present for all to see, that she was indeed once again in need of help: 'She'll have to be put away again.' Even the doctor had no name for the different woman our mother became.

All it meant in my heart was that she couldn't possibly care when she could so easily leave us to the mercy of a father whose own abusive power was totally in place by that time.

The year I began senior school was something of a landmark. After failing to be promoted in fifth class and struggling throughout sixth to prepare for the state primary school examinations, it was no mean achievement, in my eyes, to discover when the results were issued that not only had I passed the examination, but had also secured a place in my older sister's school. It was with a sense of pride that I wore my new uniform, even if sometimes I felt like 'a babe in the woods', lost and in danger. Yet the fact that I was allowed to be part of a world where there was security and adult acceptance gave me a little more confidence that there must be something good about me even when a still, small voice whispered inside me, 'but not good enough'.

---

[1] At the end of her time with me, Sister Mary discovered that her older sister had also suffered sexual abuse. But she had been able to marry and to raise a family.

As the years went on, the people I loved most seemed unable to stay in my life for long. First aunt Eileen left for England and work in Liverpool and then Nanna died. Still the will to survive grew stronger and took a firm hold in my mind. By this time I had some friends and a school life that gave me direction and teachers who seemed to be on my side, however poor my academic performance might be.

Yet one day in class, just before the date when the entrance fee for the Intermediate Certificate Exam needed to be paid, I made a decision. No longer would I plead or beg for money from my father, nor would I again tolerate the humiliation of having my name posted on the 'fees not paid' list for all to see on the school's notice-board. That very day I told the head nun that I would not be taking the exam, and the same evening I announced to my father, with a determination and defiance I had never in my life previously displayed, my intention to leave school and find a job. No amount of argument or persuasion served to move me from the position I had taken. I was never going back to school, I said, and that was final.

Within days I found a job as a shop assistant in a small store and in less than a week regretted my defiant stand but did not breathe a word of this at home.

Out of the blue, or so it seemed at the time, a hairdresser friend of my mother's offered me an apprenticeship in her city salon. That April began four of the happiest years of my life. It seemed I had a natural talent and creativity for the job and the ability to develop an easy working relationship with the clients.

But those apprenticeship years offered much more than the opportunity to develop new skills: they allowed me time and space to regain control of my life, gather together my inner resources and find the courage to dream of a future. At the time, however, I had no words to articulate such a concept.

Slowly the dream I had as a tiny girl, to one day be a nun and care for children, surfaced and as the third year of my apprenticeship drew to a close I began making plans to that end.

Mounting pressure from my father demanded I wait at least a full year before he would give his consent. But not even the understanding, and he made it very clear, that I would receive not one penny of his money to finance such a foolhardy venture, prevented or daunted me in any way. It was, I believe, *intended* to be.

It meant I had to find the money to provide a whole new wardrobe which I was required to bring along and still have enough money to buy an airline ticket: a tall order for someone earning a junior hairdresser's wage. Yet on the assigned date I was ready to leave and join the order of my choice in a convent in England. Headily, and somewhat gleefully, I bade family, friends and a confused boyfriend good-bye, bound for a new life that would in time allow me to realise my dream of caring for children in Africa. All might be well as long as I could ignore the small voice that repeatedly whispered: 'You're not good enough, who do you think you are anyway?'

Some months into my eighth year in the convent, when I had all but given up hope of ever being sent on the mission, my African assignment arrived. I danced for joy around the room in the Midlands house of our congregation.

While I waited for the red tape of visa and entry permits, vaccinations and medical to be completed, my excitement was hardly containable! When word finally came from the Mother house that we were due to arrive in Africa before Christmas and that we should arrange to visit our families prior to leaving, I was only temporarily subdued by the prospect of saying good-bye for what might be some years and quickly recovered when the instructions to return directly to the Mother house arrived. The road to my Mecca was almost in view!

And so at the end of that trip to Ireland, knowing that in all probability it would be seven whole years before I might see any of my family again, I took a blinkered and outwardly blissful leave of a family whose lives were in serious disarray. Both parents barely spoke to each other, although living under the same roof, and although two of my brothers and one sister were married by then, signs of childhood trauma that I had been taught to recognise during childcare training were very much in evidence. But because I was as yet unwilling to acknowledge the existence of any such damage, lest I too might come within the spotlight of such an admission, I left them, secretly glad to be going out of reach: a whole continent away.

Africa was the epitome of all my dreams. From the moment I arrived I was captivated by that wonderful country of contrasts and colour. The flowers, trees and mountains; the vastness of the land and the height of the sky, the like of which I had never before seen. In the evening, just before nightfall came down with a sudden darkness to turn the world to the blackest black, the sky changed to the deepest orange leaving me with the warmth of a land that would in the morning dawn again to sunshine blue. Even now these images remain in my mind's eye to gladden my heart in the hope that this beautiful country may now begin to find its way home.

But it was the people of this land who drew me like a magnet to feel that never again would I fail to be a part of their lives. Twice weekly I escaped from 'white South Africa' (the land was still then in the grip of the apartheid system), to go into the township and take time to bask in the warmth of generous-hearted people.

It was from them that I learned to understand what it is to be cherished, valued and loved. From them, too, I learned that nurturing children is of paramount importance, and the better to achieve success each member of the extended family has a significant role to play in the task of child-rearing.

I heard stories of hardship and struggle that would break the strongest spirit, but still these people had dreams of a future full of hope that would bring a better life for their children; dreams that were so often overshadowed by a quality of life that offered hardly the barest of essentials, and those essentials not worthy of the name. A tin shack to call home, a working day that began at 3a.m. and ended often at 9.30p.m. – and all for R100 monthly. But the sheer tenacity of those people, the music and colour, their joy and their peacefulness in the face of so much adversity remain to this day etched in my memory. And when at last I left their land to return to England, memories of that noble people and their spirit gave me courage to face my own dark days to come.

Although work in the 'white' area could no longer conceal that my life was beginning to show some signs of stress and even fracture, it would still be held together for a while longer by those twin towers: a supportive community with its warm and generous affirmation; and the structured, disciplined lifestyle that would keep the growing sense of emptiness at bay.

Chapter Seven

That July, news of the vote that would permit me to take my final vows to become a permanent member of the congregation reached me. On a sunny October morning, as my twin brother led the procession into the chapel, packed with our sisters, colleagues and friends, who had come, as he had done, for the ceremony, and the strains of 'Jesu Joy of Man's Desiring' reverberated throughout the building, I seemed to hear someone breathe a sigh of deep relief and a whisper: 'You've made it, that can only mean you *are* good enough!'

Yet when a new assignment demanded that I move to Natal – were they not 'sending me away'? – the 'not good enough' chant took up its incessant refrain until I could hear nothing else, and I became convinced that there was something about being accepted that would for ever remain beyond my reach. When the time came for me to leave my first African home, I went, barely able to bid anyone good-bye; too numb and empty inside for words and only able to cry for days on my arrival, yet still I could tell no one how badly I felt and how much I wished I was dead.

It was the flowers and the sheer beauty of the area that finally brought about some change. Each morning when I awoke the scent from a shrub growing just below my window floated into my room, permeating the air with a wonderful sweetness: its name was 'Yesterday, today and tomorrow', because, said the gardener, 'it goes on and on growing'. Maybe I could go on growing too, I thought. And so I eased myself cautiously into the lives of that Durban community, in time counting myself blessed indeed to be there. In the next four years I even brought some music, song and joy, some happiness into the lives of the children with whom I worked and I . took pride in their achievements and development. I put myself in their place and fended off my own desperate need for help so that I, too, might heal and grow.

While all went well the feeling of 'not being good enough' could be kept in check. But sometimes after dark, when the working day was over, I stood for a while on the veranda watching the city lights from our hilltop convent and heard the foghorn from some ship out on the bay, and that lonely sound found an echo within me and seemed to stir a lost and lonely child to the brink of awareness. But those secrets were still closed to me and at the time I was still a long way from opening my soul to that child's existence; let alone my ears to her cries for help. And so I would turn my back on the scene, dismiss the moment and, feeling infinitely sad each time, seek refuge in the next day's work.

The years passed all too quickly. Soon it was time to visit the family in Ireland. By now my view of the world was once again seen through rose-tinted glasses. Everything was wonderful ... just as long as memories could be kept at bay ... just as long as the sun shone.

Once in Ireland, with each day that I spent in that house of my childhood, the rosy tinge soon faded and it seemed I was in a house of horrors and that it was haunted. Although it was one of my mother's 'at home' times, my parents did not speak to one another and I barely saw my brothers and sisters, all of whom had by now left home. They seemed to avoid me and I was glad when the time came to get away.

At the end of that holiday I went back to Africa gladly, feeling that at least there I might be free from a panic that some end was near, where pictures from the past appeared to terrorise me. But even in Africa the shutters of my mind would no longer stay closed. Work refused to keep them under lock and key. I recognised that I had lost the knack of pretending that all was well. I became increasingly vulnerable to the dread that my secret might be exposed. As the feelings of worthlessness took hold, I began a pattern of hiding away at every opportunity. That I was seriously ill I still tried to hide from myself.

In the end I requested a change of work, a breathing space, maybe even a change of scene, perhaps in England: anything, I said, anything. Looking back as the person I am today, I can only wonder why nobody stepped in with a question there and then. Did I give such a signal of 'hands off' by keeping myself to myself in such fear?

Back in England, where I settled in our Manchester convent, the G.P. recommended that I see a psychiatrist. He feared that I was seriously depressed, quite a new word for myself, and provided 'first aid' by way of some antidepressants. Dr Smith, together with my mother superior Sister Hilda, got me through some scary times when I always feared the worst but without knowing what that worst might be. Later, when it seemed that I had recovered and after brief counselling in the Dympha Centre that, with hindsight, was sadly not equipped to understand or touch the place where my deeper trouble lay – the core of my disintegration, I was allowed to return to my work in Africa to my immeasurable relief; for it felt like divine approval and forgiveness. Yet warnings of what lay ahead I had, in the usual way, swept under the carpet encouraged by professionals who should have known better.

Three years later, when I heard that my parents had finally separated and at the same time found myself confronted by two little girls severely sexually abused by their father, and who had to be taken into a place of safety under the terms of the then Children's Act in South Africa, my whole world simply unravelled and I suffered a serious breakdown that must have been waiting in the wings for most of my life.

Yet again I quickly got myself back into counselling and had two six-week periods of hospitalisation in a clinic, when I would have nothing to do with the local mental hospital. But even if the doctors patched me up I could no longer fool myself that the 'recovery' was more than temporary each time. Finally, as an act of desperation I took the law into my own hands and requested leave of absence from the congregation. It seemed I must be too much for everyone, although in reality I was supported and surrounded by immense kindness and warmth from my community. Yet feeling that I did not deserve it I simply could not take it in.

Finally, too ill and broken-hearted to carry on, I left Africa for England in mufti, with very little will left to continue the fight for life. Again my aunt came to the rescue. Her mothering and care put me back on my feet once more. Even if there were temporary set-backs when I would plunge into despair and want to give the struggle up I managed to work for two years in a boarding school as matron, once again giving the care to children I needed so badly for myself, and when I felt ready, I returned to where I knew I belonged: to the religious life and to our convent. Even then, a long way still lay ahead before I was to find the courage to face the lonely, damaged child that hid with such determination, still under lock and key, in some compartment of my mind.

This time my assignment was to one of our convents in Ireland. I found myself in constant conflict with my superior about something or other, but mostly about procedural and management issues; and when it became obvious that I could no longer remain objective in casework, I was withdrawn from the field and offered a desk job in our London convent.

When I arrived Sister Jan was there, a familiar face from my days in Africa, now matron of our convent's nursing home. Her joyful, warm welcome was a much-needed lifeline. And when summer arrived and I had become transparently pale and painfully thin, it was she who insisted that I contact Dr Fernandes for a second time. Fibroids and anaemia were diagnosed, followed by blood tests and a scan; and there would need to be a hysterectomy.

When I was home again and the endometriosis Dr V. had discovered during surgery was also cleared away, I went on a late autumn holiday, feeling well, happy, free and clean ... cleaner than I had done for years. But it was the very 'clean' feeling, so painfully undeserved, that brought me to Sister Jan one day to tell her how very wrong everything was: a life under false pretences that I knew I could no longer face.

It was a move that would turn out to be the richest and best of all blessings. It would lead me to the 'red door' where the lady lived, in search of help. In time, when I was able to call her by name and had learned to trust and then even to love her, Dr Nini Herman had become a friend and had built from the frozen scrap I brought to her on that first day, a person, full of life and love, ready for life 'on the open road'.

Accordingly it came about that on a January day, early in the frozen year, my life's real work had begun.

Chapter Eight

It was halfway through the first year of my weekly Thursday session and we were fast approaching the first long summer break. More disturbed than I yet knew at the prospect of the long separation, I boarded the wrong bus as I considered this, my last visit for what seemed an eternity.

I telephoned the lady to explain what had happened, and was relieved when she said, 'Why not come anyway, we will still have some time, even 15 minutes'. The bitterness of separation was slightly sweetened by her reassurance and understanding and as I left the lady's house for the first long summer holiday, feeling she might even be on my side, I was able to enjoy two weeks in Scotland with a certain sense of freedom. This relief did not last.

Once back in London, as the late summer dragged into autumn each Thursday I felt frustrated and angry for it seemed that I might never see the lady again. I would drive down her road and the sight of her car outside her home gave me courage to hold on a little longer until the beginning of term.

When the first day of the new term finally arrived, I drove the short distance by car, but I felt so intimidated by the presence of the children near the only available parking space that I drove off fuming at my 'foolishness'; what made me so afraid of the strained, neglected faces of those children? Had someone abandoned them? Inside the house, another 'foolishness' stopped me in my tracks – someone had been sitting in 'my' chair! This is my room, I thought, and nobody ever told me others came here too.

Nervous and tight, afraid that the lady might know what I was thinking, I took my place with a sigh and waited for the 'little girl' who lives inside me to emerge, as she did now sometimes in the safety of that room. Sister Mary, polite, proper, correct and, above all, good, also came each time. It seemed that she was in charge, yet she stayed on the fringe of things, always at a distance, ever watchful, just in case. She was angry too, and fearful, ever ready to take over. Nor did she have time for the 'cry baby' who was always making trouble, and had to be watched.

'You have no compassion for the "little girl" with the broken toys and unfinished dolly clothes', I heard the lady say time and again, seeming to be reproachful. 'You don't expect anyone to have regard for you or feel any warmth towards you.' It seemed so true and very sad but still there was a 'cry baby' somewhere, if only I could find why it was she cried. Whatever might be troubling her was all so very long ago, buried still in pain and time.

Once I had told the lady, in single words here and there, why it was I had come, for weeks and months of each session I sat on 'my' settee wrapped in my coat, hands hidden, but could find no words to tell her of the despair and helplessness that seemed to engulf me so that I became tongue-tied and could only sit there in hopeless silence, feeling that I might never be allowed to escape from that awful 'haunted house' of my childhood.

Later that autumn, nearing the end of the first year, after much negotiation and with the silent fear that I was asking too much of my congregation and the lady, I agreed that it was in my interest to come more than just once a week. On the first occasion of a second weekly session, I went along with a sort of foreboding, not in the least surprised to find no less than six 'for sale' signs in the street. Then, when I discovered there was no light in the hallway, I was very relieved to see the lady appear at the door, for I had feared she might have left. 'You don't use your eyes or common sense. The bulb has gone and needs to be replaced, and the signs say "flat for sale". You are afraid that your demands will wear me out and will drive me away,' the lady said, and it seemed she was comforting a frightened, tearful child who had woken from some bad dream. 'You never expect to be taken care of. You expect that I will leave you, as your mother did each time she was taken ill again. Perhaps you felt responsible and that you were too much for her.'

On another occasion, the lady said: 'You haven't really put your-self in my hands. You are still expecting me to take advantage of you. You don't really trust people.' How was it she knew all this, for it was all too true, I thought. All I could talk about on that day was how much I was making a fuss and being a nuisance; of the need to stay quiet and not ask too many questions, in case I should be sent away, to an orphanage no doubt.

During the following months feelings of abandonment and isolation surfaced with increasing intensity and when words came I spoke only of people leaving me, of some girl who had no place to go when her children's home refused to have her back after she had staged a second failed suicide attempt; and how lonely it was without a family, now that even my youngest sister, K., had rejected me in the aftermath of my disclosure. 'You feel you have no place here or anywhere,' the lady repeated at intervals. 'You cut yourself off from everyone, from the very thought of contacting, let alone visiting, her.' But I shook my head at that suggestion and would give no reply to her kind, 'No?'

The very next time I came I told her, or rather flung at her in an I-told-you-so sort of voice, that my sister had no wish to have contact with me now or ever, and had told me so that very morning on the telephone. I went straight on to talk about being sent to England for a holiday the year I was nine years old, as though it were some sort of punishment, when in reality it was a privilege. 'You felt your mother wanted rid of you, maybe even wanted you dead,' said the lady.

'Yes, that was it,' I replied, feeling afraid and remembering a crystal flower vase flying through the air which my mother had once thrown at my father, or was it at me?

'That's about broken virginity,' she said.

Early in the second year anger began to emerge that was very frightening, and I was horrified by the intensity of the violent feelings I harboured towards my father, but I was as yet unwilling to verbally detail the abuse no matter how often the lady encouraged me in that direction. I would protest angrily and in tears about feeling I was being pushed to divulge something so secret; then, instantly, become withdrawn, fearful that after such an outburst, I would be sent back to that dreadful house and I would cower in a far and distant corner of my mind because it seemed some awful damage had been inflicted by me on the lady. When I was able to take things in again, it was to be confronted by the way I withdrew: 'You are afraid to come closer to me. You feel that your angry feelings have the power to destroy me; that I will send you back to the dreadful house to be hurt again by your father every time your mother is back in hospital.'

I left that day tearful and very upset. How was it, I asked myself over and over, that she knew all these things when I never once dared even to think them in her presence?

When I was ready to leave and came out into the hallway the front door opened so that I came face to face with a lady I had seen many times on the street near the red door. We had exchanged nods

by way of greeting and sometimes even said 'hello' as we passed. If I
suspected she too came to see the lady, I never once acknowledged it.
But now like a frightened cornered animal, I fled through the door in
consternation and sheer panic.

'It seems you have to share me too, as you did your mother with
your twin,' said the lady when I told her.

'Yes, that's exactly it,' I said in wonder and surprise. 'And she
loved him so very much. Even when she was dying it was B. she had
wanted. He made her laugh, she always said.'

'You fear you might now be too much for me and I might want to
replace you with other babies, with an amusing boy.' And I nodded,
with a tiny smile, for I was, I think, still ashamed of the 'baby talk' the
lady used as if we were in a nursery.

Chapter Nine

I was still obsessed with people leaving me when election time came around that year and a poster supporting the Labour Party appeared in the lady's window. It seemed that she, too, had left me to go over to my father's 'side'. Even worse, the consulting room window was boarded up with wood. Had he perhaps laid siege to the house? As I approached the red door I was filled with a feeling of trepidation, suspecting some mine to explode at any moment. Once inside the room, which was in obvious disarray, I made no mention of this fact nor voiced the sense of danger I felt hanging on the air, thinking that to do so would be only to make unnecessary fuss. The only concession I made to my worries was to say, 'My father supported the Labour Party and my mother always said he was a communist.'

The lady picked up on my increased vulnerability, saying, 'You seem to feel this is a very dangerous place now, yet you have not mentioned that the window is boarded up or the state of the room; you don't feel entitled to comment on anything.' An intruder had broken in, she explained. 'This awakens feelings of dangerous and painful intrusion in you. A fear that you do not know how to protect yourself.'

On the way home that evening danger of some unknown kind seemed to lurk in every doorway and on each street corner. That night I had a dream. Two friendly people approached me, one of whom it seemed I knew, and taking me by the hand, said, 'come along little one, it will be all right now'. It was followed by the return of a dream I periodically had over many years: a horrible black thing came after me. I felt totally beyond the pale and said there was a heaviness in my chest which brought the depression days so much to mind.

'No sooner do you feel safe and protected with me than something horrible and frightening threatens you,' said the lady. 'You don't keep me inside as a good supporting person.' What a strange thing to say over and over. And whatever did she mean by that? I thought as I went home. How can anyone be kept inside?

Next time, hardly seated, I said in a this-is-an-announcement tone used by radio and TV newscasters, that Terry Waite was taking time off to write his autobiography and wasn't that wonderful? Though her voice was as quiet and gentle as before, she said: 'Perhaps you feel he is giving you permission to tell me your life story fully.'

I still felt that she was cross. I searched her face but found there not the slightest sign that she might be annoyed. Had she not encouraged me to keep a diary; 'Perhaps one day you will write your autobiography,' she had said. I smiled each time, pleased by her belief in such a possibility, yet shook my head whenever the question arose. I had no words, could hardly spell; besides, she might even want to read what I had written and words were such dangerous things, and how then could I write, I thought.

'You refuse to think of yourself as creative,' the lady said, and I could feel myself shrink, Alice-like, and become small; it seemed that I was back in that house, silent and without a voice. As the weeks passed I found it more and more difficult to speak at all, until a day came when I was mute. No single word would cross my lips.

The Labour Party poster, still in the window, caught my eye as I neared the red door, and I froze. My father was there, it seemed, and now what was I to do? That painting of 'the devil man' I sometimes called 'my warehouse dream' in which I had left him shut inside that sinister building as it burned! Had I not left him inside that building as it burned? I saw him, here at the window, in the glow as I crept down the steps, let myself very quietly into the house and was vastly relieved when, after the familiar wood-on-carpet sound of the door, the lady herself appeared, and not my father.

'Your angry feelings towards your father feel so powerful that you believe they could burn him down. You would also like to burn me down when you feel resentful that other babies come here.' It seemed I did not like the sound of 'resentful' either, and then I heard my father, 'him', say 'goody two shoes' mockingly, as he always mocked me, and I was very frightened.

'You don't keep me inside as a good supporting person', she said. How can I? I silently threw back at her, when if I but blink you disappear.

Some short time afterwards, I brought another dream to one of the sessions. I said it was an open space which I described as a 'clearing site where children were at play'. The lady asked what it was I thought I saw in it, and although I have no recall as to my response, I wrote in my diary that the lady seemed pleased, for she said 'perhaps it is a long time since you played, carefree, in a clearing site'.

My fear of madness grew less and I was better able to explore the mystery of my grandfather's illness. I had only seen him once in my life, when we had been visiting my mother who was in hospital. At her insistence I was taken with her to see this mysterious grandfather who was, I was told, 'in the other building', a huge barracks of a place. I remember feeling very frightened; as I told the lady, it seemed to me that my mother was saying, 'look, here is the reason for all that has happened to me'.

Following that session, the very next day in fact, I phoned the hospital where both my grandfather and my mother had spent so much of their lives. I explained that I was 'in therapy' and that I would appreciate any information that might throw light on my mother's childhood to facilitate some understanding of her condition. After some discussion the social worker told me she would contact me soon with whatever information she could find. I could hardly wait for the next session to tell the lady.

In telling her, I called her by her name the first time. I wrote a single word: 'good' beside the entry in my diary. 'Nini, I phoned the hospital.' She wondered what the reason was. I said it was an effort to get my life back on track. Nini responded with a big warm smile and I was glad. It seemed that I had cleared a stack of files from my desk and was well satisfied with my work that day.

There still lay months of work ahead of us that would be dogged with awful silences from time to time, but now that I could at last call her by name, Nini had become a real person and it seemed we had changed gear to climb a very steep hill.

As my commitment to my healing developed, and I had turned down the opportunity to work on a tiny island in the Pacific to continue in therapy, some other fears emerged. What would happen when I was dismantled and when the scaffolding came down? Who would be left? And however would I cope?

Some of the answers to these questions were not long in coming. When Nini, Mother General and Jan all had holidays that coincided that year, I felt that my 'scaffolding', without warning, had been taken down and it seemed I had been abandoned once more by all the 'adults': I felt I might die.

By some miracle, I survived that episode and then, when it was time for Jan's return, I phoned Nini in great distress one night: 'Jan would be home tomorrow' I said, 'but I had done so very well in her absence and would she now not be furious?'

'You feel that I would withhold support once you feel stronger,' Nini suggested at the next session. Hardly had we finished our work on that, when yet another obstacle replaced it, for Sister Jan's new assignment arrived that would take her to the other end of the country. Clearly she could not stand my progress.

Now I reported dreams that were full of rage: white cups smashed by somebody lay in smithereens at my feet. I complained that people continued to leave me. 'You feel', Nini said, 'that you have nothing good to offer that might make any of us want to stay. You are attacking me for abandoning you to sexual abuse from your father when I should have been there to protect you.'

This shed some light on the proceedings, but as the months went on the 'Mafia's' silencing tactics continued until, session by session, I could no longer speak. Even Nini's suggestion that I was under orders from a dangerous father not to speak did not seem to help. Then Nini discovered a vehicle that would facilitate our journey, and that was easily at our disposal.

'Why not paint a picture of the house and bring it here,' she said one day. She told me of an art therapy group she had once supervised in her lunch-time at the hospital where she had formerly worked and what a useful tool it had proved to be. She felt it might help our work. Seeing that I could not speak, frozen by some inner terror, by some fatal prohibition, we had nothing to lose.

During the summer I began to paint. Each painting spoke eloquently and with startling clarity of the trauma I had endured and of the terror I was unable still to fully verbalise.

And as the trapdoors and the shutters of my mind stayed open a little longer each time I brought another painting, I would listen while Nini helped me to make some sense of the meanings they might hold. Gradually the terror minimised and an understanding grew that I was no longer that helpless unprotected child and need no longer run or hide.

We worked steadfastly for some more months and survived several attempts on my part either to reduce the sessions or to bring the therapy to a hasty termination, when it seemed I was either too greedy, too demanding or needed to placate the 'adults' and, also, when the pain seemed unbearable; above all, when the terror grew that my father would attack, possibly murder me, if I divulged his evil ways to any other person.

Still the 'beyond the pale' feelings persisted and when the third year of therapy was under way and Jan left for her new post, I was filled with an unspeakable sense of hopelessness. Had my mother gone into hospital again, and what had me in this tiny brace-like grip I asked myself, overwhelmed by despair, feeling that I was back in that dreadful house again, from which there would now be no escape. 'You feel too guilty towards your mother to escape when she was not able to get away,' I heard Nini say, and it was true.

I was in church with the community for evening prayer when the phone call came on the Tuesday evening; it was Nini. 'I have been watching Maya Angelou, the American poet, being interviewed on television', she said, 'and I could not stop thinking about you. She was raped by her father, mute for five whole years afterwards, and, she told the interviewer, "Here I am risen from all that and now I will read from the steps of Capitol Hill!". Keep that vision before you,' Nini said.

When I put the phone down it seemed someone had found the way to that dreadful house and that I was no longer alone and forgotten. Hope had once again been restored.

Shortly after this I borrowed a book written by Nini from the library and wrote the following lines from it on one side of a card, which I carry with me to this day:

> ... we have gained new qualities of calm and growing inner strength which we did not possess before and a partner at our side; presently, this partner will find a place within our heart, someone with whom to face whatever comes, knowing that we will not be spared the ordeal of psychic pain, but that we will not be written off in frightening or malicious ways, as may have been the case in our infantile experience ..."[1]

So that was what she meant each time she reminded me I was not keeping her inside as a good supporting person; a partner in the uphill struggle.

---

[1] Nini Herman (1987). *Why Psychotherapy*. Free Association Books, London, p.72.

Chapter Ten

As the painting progressed and I was able to bring along 'nice' work for Nini to see, she said one day that she would like to show some of my paintings to her husband, who was an artist. While it pleased me greatly that she should show such interest, still I hesitated, and only after several months when she raised it as a possibility again did I find the courage to accept the invitation and called Mr Herman to set up an appointment.

It was 1.40p.m., Thursday afternoon, when I set out, paintings in hand, for the meeting with Josef Herman and it seemed as if I was going to a birthday party! Still there lurked in a corner of my mind a fear, or was it fear?: I could not quite say, but it seemed as though I told a small child when she started to fuss: 'Stop it now, that is enough nonsense for today!'

This time I mounted steps to another red door and could hear the bell, when I pushed it, ring a friendly tone inside the house and soon the sound of slippered feet approached the door. It was opened wide by a small man, yet he appeared like a giant; or was it my mother or the 'flower lady', and my Nanna too? All three seemed to appear at once. He greeted me with a 'Come in, come in' and a warm handshake and directed me before him to a small alcove sort of room. But had I boarded a ship, I asked myself, for steep wooden steps led down to the highest of rooms, the likes of which I had never in my life seen before.

In a flash and from the corner of my eye I saw it and froze. A bed dressed in dark colours: was my father here too? I stood riveted to the ground in paralysed terror unable to move a step. Danger took my breath away.

'Go on, go on' his voice behind me said. Half-turning, I saw the man pointing to the stairway: 'down there' he said. I moved, trance-like, carefully down the stairs away from the shadows, out of danger, just in the nick of time.

I felt instantly dwarfed by the room's height, but this room had light in it. Did it come from the skylight windows high above? I wasn't sure. But I, like Alice, gazed in wonder at all that was to be seen. Paints and brushes, wood and frames stacked against the walls. Huge, towering pictures, reds and oranges, yellows and blacks and blues. This I felt, was no Alice-land. Things here were solid, tangible and true. In this wonderland I knew I would be safe.

A little girl emerged from hiding to sit beside me on the space the man had cleared for me. We both listened quietly while he spoke once he had seated himself in his armchair.

'Put your paintings over there and let us talk awhile,' said Mr Herman. I gladly and easily answered his questions. It seemed I had known him all my life, or maybe a long time ago. And then when he had looked at my work, this gracious man spoke of commitment, love and dedication as the very hallmarks of any artist and the need to follow what's in the heart and then of the importance of tenacity in the face of opposition or obstacles. He spoke of St John of the Cross and of St Teresa and of the sheer simplicity and beauty of his daughter Becci's poem, written long ago: 'It rains and I cry!'

He went on to speak of Sean O'Casey and George Bernard Shaw and of Ireland – and he stressed the importance of drawing on one's own resources. 'That is what painting is all about, expressing what is within.' Had I been on some retreat, maybe even spoken with the Pope? There was so much goodness here.

'And now we shall have some tea?' It was a question and I thanked him and said that would be very nice and went before him up the wooden stairs, only now a little girl held my hand and we seemed to disembark from some long voyage. When we had finished tea in a nearby café and I bade him good-bye, I knew my life would be for ever enriched by that meeting with him, for he had helped me find something I had lost long ago: a trust in my good father of my early childhood years.

Chapter Eleven

Now it was March. After every session I was angry with Nini, yet it seemed incomprehensible. What in heaven's name was happening? It seemed that nothing Nini did or did not do was right.

While we navigated the hostile waters of my anger, and as I tried to make some sense of it all, I finally raised these feelings with her, for I could no longer deny their presence or my growing hostility. Increasingly upset, I spoke of my father's dismissive attitude towards my mother and of doctors who had shown a lack of insight or interest in my mother's plight.

'Perhaps you feel that I dismiss your pain and difficulties and show no compassion,' Nini suggested. 'And we are approaching the Easter break.'

Small comfort, I thought as I went home. What happens if you can't sustain the pressure and what if I lose your support and if I lose you too as I lost my mother ... what then? So our journey inched forward and she did indeed seem to be up to withstanding everything that came her way and I felt she was always there for me.

Gradually, as the concept of compassion dawned and found a home in me, I was able to extend it to others so that when two young boys beat a very small child to death, I said to Nini, 'Something must have happened in their young lives to make them behave in such a way.'

'You wouldn't have said that this time last year!' was Nini's reply.

It seemed I could take things in more frequently, even if I still felt responsible for others in incomprehensible ways. Yet a faint hope in the right to a life of my own, away from that 'house of horrors', slowly found its way into my mind. I began to make plans for the future; the promise of a fresh start in America was enough to keep my new-found hope alive during the coming months.

'We will be finished by July,' I told Nini when next we met.

'You are afraid of getting too much out of it,' she replied.

That weekend I had three dreams:

I could see a huge festering sore, it seemed to me; I was very frightened and asked someone: 'would it ever heal?'.

The second dream: it was war-time; I could see the bombing of an entire city and then a bewildered, devastated man looking for his family.

The third dream: I was being thrown out of a house; you were there, I told Nini, at first just standing by, then there was a sense of you being there in a supportive kind of way.

My first thought when I woke was: will I never see her again if I go to America? Again, I grew silent, this time with a dreadful fear.

'You were afraid that your mother would retaliate, would bomb you and throw you out of the house. It seems that you feel that I have become a dangerous retaliating mother,' Nini said quietly.

We agreed on that occasion that it ought to be my responsibility to negotiate ongoing therapy to the end of that year and Nini acknowledged she had been wrong to ask Dr Fernandes to do so on my behalf. 'It could', she said, 'seem that I didn't trust you to take care of yourself and I am sorry.'

At the following session, Nini asked if she had told me her holiday dates: I gave a little nod and she continued, 'And you know I will not be working on bank holiday Monday.'

I had, of course, remembered this, but had not allowed myself to think about it nor accept it in the here and now. But I was furious and said no word of it to Nini that day.

'I have been painting the cliffs again,' I said. 'Sometimes it seems I still go up there.'

'That is when there is a separation,' came the reply.

I agreed: 'It's like being back in that house,' I said. 'It's like walking through a dark part of the Licky Hills in Birmingham. There are people all around but I feel alone and vulnerable and very frightened.'

Nini paraphrased some lines from Robert Frost's poem: '... the woods are lonely dark and deep', and I silently added: 'And I have promises to keep and miles to go before I sleep ...' I knew then there was a long way still to go.

When I got home that afternoon, a card from the library had arrived. It said the book, *My Kleinian Home*, Nini's autobiographical account of four psychotherapies, was ready for collection. Filled with fright, delight and panic, I went to the library to pick it up, and sat on one of the library window-seats to read it. I held the book with immense reverence as though it were my Office Book[1].

When I got home I continued to read it late into the night. I was so moved by the story of heartbreaking sorrow and then filled with such admiration for her tenacity to keep going in the face of so much suffering, that I wrote the following poem, entitled 'Beacon Light', and promised that should I ever write my own book, I would use those words as a tribute to Nini Herman.

Beacon Light
A tribute to Doctor Nini Herman.

I read continuously through the night,
Kept vigil near the holy ground.
Cried, laughed and cried again.
And it seemed I would die of that dire
Pain unfolding there before my eyes.
But when once more she seemed to rise,
Inspired by the Kleinian Way,
I closed my eyes to sleep a while,
Only to dream of padded cells,
Rustle of starched cloth, broken lives,
And pain that would not go away.
Two more hours in daytime light
Took up a second vigil watch,
Read and watched in wonder great,
As out of heartbreak grew
A Beacon Light which would with time
Serve as guide for those in need,
And lead, out of the darkest wood,
Into a light,
And point to the Open Road.
April 2, 1993.

On the following Saturday I had a dream: I was in a doctor's surgery and the doctor seemed to be you, Nini. She wanted to take a closer look at something that clearly needed attention. 'No, please don't touch it, doctor,' I said, 'it's too sore', But the doctor continued to examine the tender area while I repeatedly moved out of reach. I awoke in great distress, and when again I went to sleep I dreamed a second time: You came to our house for the session, Nini, only it wasn't you, but she had your voice. A lady with white wavy hair and glasses. A bit like Nanna but still tall, like you, and with your voice but slightly stooped. We sat in our community room but throughout

---

[1]Book of prescribed prayers, services and meditations.

the session I was worried. Towards the end you asked what I usually did at this time and asked when I prayed; and what I intended to do about my untidy room. Some children came into the room at this point, and we seemed to be standing at the rails of a balcony. You waved to the children. You took from your bag three books: painting books; a large, a medium and a smaller, oblong one. Your face was on the cover of the medium one. 'There, you didn't know I could paint. This will teach you how to use colours,' you said.

'Is the room untidy with the conflict of whether it is safe to take a closer look here, at much that is still unsaid and painful. That which needs to be painted in words this time?' Nini asked after a while.

On the following Monday I brought some flowers which I had gathered in our garden and had made into a little arrangement. I was very nervous about giving these, but Nini received them with obvious pleasure and I was pleased. 'Someone is bringing a camera tonight. I'm going to take a photograph of them. Would you like a copy?' That photograph sits on my desk as I type.

The following Thursday I reported feeling that my whole body was in pain. And how orphaned I felt at weekends and breaks. How very much I wanted to see Ireland again.

'You want to go home,' Nini said.

'But there is other pain, the pain of feeling angry with you: a good, kind lady who understands suffering, who can show appreciation, is interested and shows concern in all kinds of different ways. So why this feeling of neglect when it is time for weekends and holidays? I don't quite understand,' I said.

'You feel unappreciated and neglected if I don't give you all my time and attention,' came the reply – and it was true.

Soon after this episode a letter arrived giving me freedom to continue therapy and telling me to be guided by Nini as to the timing of its termination. Further, the assignment to America would still be made available to me when I was ready. I was euphoric with relief and gave the letter to Nini to read the very next time I saw her.

'Yes, but you never expect to have anyone respond to you warmly', she said, 'to meet your needs.'

We talked then about a dream I had had about going to Ireland with a one-way ticket. 'So, you no longer want the security of a return ticket,' Nini said. 'You are afraid of exhausting me and want to get out before I fall sick, like your mother.'

I told her how much I longed to walk along the river bank, to see the 'flower lady', to have my brothers and sisters with me. Then I said, 'Mother General thinks I may become too dependent on you.'

'Dependence is the high road to independence,' she replied.

I smiled, very close to tears, feeling so affirmed. On that note we ended the term. Nini held out her hand and this time I was able to take it and gave her a little hug. I left with a sense that I had been entrusted with the care of something precious and that I could be counted on to take seriously that responsibility for care and protection of myself.

Chapter Twelve

I had worked in the other house of our congregation, on the outskirts of London, during the break, and enjoyed the days of solitude in peaceful, pastoral surroundings, sometimes reading under a beautiful oak tree serenaded by birdsong or standing a while on the riverbank to watch swans or boats glide gracefully by. I wrote in my diary: 'I've come back to the essence of my childhood and I'm here on the Shannon River.' Enormous planes roared overhead from time to time on their descent route to Heathrow airport and although I looked up in awe, I ignored the disturbance that the sound created in my inner world.

New problems soon lay in wait. There was a telephone message from Nini to say she was ill and would not be able to resume work until the 6th of May. I burst into tears, to my embarrassment, right there in my office before my colleagues. How could I tell them my mother had once more gone and left me and that I might never see her again; that she may even die!

When we met again in May, I was terribly distraught and filled with conflicting emotions. I was tearful throughout the session, yet she was still there, and I was so relieved. The anger that she had left me all alone, and the certainty that it was all my fault because I had been given more time to draw closer, was confirmed by my deep-seated belief that everyone I ever loved would leave me.

As we worked our way through that forest of despair and my fears of my own destructiveness, it seemed we together reassembled a child's building of bricks that some destructive being had broken down. As I began to slowly recover from the psychological and the physical shock of being left alone and orphaned, Nini one day said: 'When I was ill I became the mother you had damaged by taking father away and leaving her without support.' And it felt all too true.

On the last day of May my focus turned to names! 'My mother couldn't even give me a name of my own, it had to be a variation of my sister's. You hardly ever call me by my name either, you probably don't even know it!' And I ranted on in this vein. After a pause I asked, 'Why am I so cross with you today?'

'You have been like this ever since I have been ill, not just today!' Nini said.

'Yes, I know,' I said, 'but will it ever change? Why do I feel so bad and so much worse now?' I asked.

'It feels worse because you are more in touch with your feelings; with the anxieties of equating me with the mother you felt you had damaged, when you heard of my illness.'

'But I am back on the cliff top again ... the little girl ...'

'And what is she feeling?'

I heard Nini say the word 'suicide', linked to the cliff top and my feelings of guilt; I interrupted her, saying 'I don't want to hear that.'

'Are you feeling you might throw yourself off the cliffs?'

'Yes,' I said. 'But I am afraid that when I say things like that you won't want anything more to do with me.'

'This image of the retaliating and damaged mother is the Achilles' heel of the whole issue. It leads you to feeling guilt and expecting abandonment until it seems better to be dead. Not that you wish to die, but because you see no way out. You don't expect to change.'

Thinking how much I had changed already, amazingly, hope returned once more.

'I think I can go home now,' I suggested.

'That's the very first time you have ever said that in the context of Ireland!' Nini said. 'And maybe there is a safe home in yourself now.'

'I feel as though I have been on a very long journey,' I said.

'Well,' came the response, 'from the cliff top to home is a very long way!'

'I've written another poem, "The Gentle Lady".' When that statement was greeted with silence, I went on: 'It's about what's happened to me during the two-and-a-half years ... I would have liked to have brought it to you, but I was frightened.'

'Why?'

'I don't know,' I replied, rather too quickly. And then, in a quiet tone after a pause, I said: 'Yes, I do, I think I'm drawing closer to you.'

'And that seems dangerous?' Nini asked.

'Yes, everyone I begin to love goes away,' I said after a long pause.

Then it seemed, out of the blue, 'I'm cross with you Nini.'

'You felt that I did not reciprocate your loving feelings.'

I gave a little nod.

'Your father was not loving towards your mother,' Nini said.

Tears filled my eyes, 'Yes, I always thought that if that was how adults behaved towards each other I didn't want to grow up.'

There was a comforting silence for some time and then I said: 'I feel as though I've been to hospital and I am just out and recovering.'

'Convalescing.'

'Yes,' I said.

'You seem to be saying no more work for a while. You would like a rest. You would like me to say that you have earned it!'

The Gentle Lady

The slightest creak of a loose floorboard
Heralds the arrival of the Gentle Lady,
As the door opens with a hint of reluctance
To the sound of wood-on-carpet, and then,
There the Gentle Lady stands, regally tall,
A tiny smile just reaching her dark, kindly eyes
Gives silent welcome,
'Do come in' it seems to say,
'I'm so pleased you have come.'
The message always the same,
Draws me ever closer to the world, where
Warmth, trust, love and even friendship
Become, not just sounds
Echoing in some chamber of an empty heart,
But concepts, full of promise,
Rays of hope that shed light and even warmth
On a soul emerging from the cold grey mist
Of a long winter's night.
This hope, fragile still but growing,
Tended through two long winters,
Weeded and nourished in spring time,
And now on the brink of summer
Reaches out with small tottering steps
Towards the Gentle Lady,
And then ... who knows ... beyond ...
To a life I too can call my very own.
2 June 1993

The next time I was due for a session I came face to face with the other lady, only now I didn't feel the need to run and hide, but felt a little sad for she seemed, I thought, upset and rather angry and there was sorrow in me that I was unable to talk to her. Nini wondered if perhaps I felt the need to have someone go with me to Ireland for protection. I acknowledged that I would like her to come with me; someone to hold my hand, for we had talked about my booking a ticket and where I was going to stay. 'I can hardly keep my eyes open I'm so tired,' I said.

'You feel they cannot accept you in Ireland as you are now, and you want to go back to dreamland where there is no more pain,' Nini said.

I was hardly out of the red door when I heard the bolt scrape into place behind me and I was very frightened. It felt like a rejection by the whole world.

When I arrived the next time, I said I had written to my family in Ireland telling them I would soon be home and now I was very worried awaiting their reply.

'Maybe you feel the women in the family might murder you on behalf of your mother.'

I told Nini how frightened I had been by the sound of the bolt on my last visit. It reminded me, I said, of the door at home. That same sound meant that my father was in. It was both terrifying and a relief.

'You expect your father to lock you out. You have no experience of being loved and cherished for yourself. There are times when you still feel beyond the pale.'

'Yes, that is true. My aunt used to say that I was like the daughter she never had, but I always wondered how that could be when I didn't even know how to be a daughter, that is to say, of course, since father ...'

'That's the problem here; you don't trust that I care ... that you are a cherished and loved daughter here, with me!'

I was very moved at this and dared not look up. I began to cry.

'You have never been able to cry at home and could never show your pain and now you're worried that they won't understand the suffering you've been through.'

The next evening I received a telephone call from Ireland. It seemed it wouldn't be in my interest to go there at present. It might be best to wait a while ... a few more months ... maybe a year.

I cancelled my flight that evening and again without consultation; although I desperately wanted to see Nini there and then, I could not bring myself to phone her. Everything seemed to be once more in little pieces at my feet. When Monday arrived I could do little else than cry during the session. Nini was very supportive, but I left in tears. The next day, Tuesday, I needed to phone her, for I feared that the whole world had stopped.

'You feel that the pain of your disappointment may be too much for you,' she said. 'And you feel that you are being a nuisance.'

'Exactly.'

'The pain of a lifetime of rejection has hit you in one big lump. Phone me tomorrow if you need to talk,' she said.

Over the next few weeks we worked our way out of that maze. Soon it was time for the long summer break and I was sad and petulant that she was going away again. Still I was able to handle it better this time, but when she returned I could talk only of separation and people leaving and how sad it would be.

'Do you perhaps feel that you may never see me again once you go to America?'

'Yes, I'm afraid so,' I said. 'Your children are lucky.'

'So are you.'

That was so comforting. It felt as though I had been given a big hug.

The next time I arrived for a session I took up the change in relationship.

'I'm not at all sure I'm ready to stop being a little girl ... it seems I've only been so for a very short time ... I don't think I want to leave it yet!' Still we continued our work and I found in October, which was the twenty-fifth anniversary of my religious profession, that a spring seemed to creep into my life bringing with it a freshness and a sense that great goodwill existed around me. The idea seeped deeper into my mind of a world where there was a place for me and where endless possibilities awaited. Finally I felt called to take up the challenge to live life to the full on my 'open road'. It seemed to me that our internal stock-taking had unearthed a treasure-house of creativity; and, as I soon discovered, the capacity to give and receive love with a joyfulness I hardly knew was possible.

We continued our work together for six more months until it was time for me to leave for America. And still I encountered some obstacles that required tenacity, skill and much attention to detail from Nini. But the understanding grew and consolidated in my mind that the foundation we had laid together was solid and sure. It was based on a firm belief that there was now someone 'at home' whom we had seen evolve from the frozen scrap encountered on that first visit to Nini. Although the frame may appear sometimes fragile; as wobbly as children's building bricks, and needing repair from time to time when my security is threatened, still it would survive, if I would but wait patiently, as I had been taught, and ride out whatever storm might come my way. And there was surety that the partner who had remained by my side on the long, hard trail from the cliff top would now be carried for ever in my heart.

Thursday 16 May, 1994
Awoke this morning with a sense that this is an important day. Sunlight streaming in through my window ... so much light now in my life and then it dawned on me ... I will be saying good-bye to Nini today. Dressed slowly and quietly reflected on the whole four years I've known her. How very fortunate I have been and what riches she has brought into my life.

'I didn't come by car today,' I told her when we met. 'I wanted to walk down the street. It no longer feels dangerous and the poor children no longer frighten me. I feel so many different things: sad, happy, glad, proud and so free.'

'There was a time when you couldn't have mixed feelings!' Nini told me.

'I wanted to say good bye to the other lady. I've grown to feel a warmth towards her; I used to feel my brother was present when we met and sometimes I was positively rude to her ...'

'Did you see the *Fiddler on the Roof?*' Nini asked. I nodded. 'When the father was seeing his daughter off to Siberia and as the train pulled out of the station he said, "God, give her warm clothes".' I smiled and nodded, understanding; and was very touched.

I said: 'I feel so much warmth, goodwill and love now. It doesn't matter if I make mistakes or am less than perfect!'

'That's because you can give love as well as being able to receive it,' Nini said. I talked about Sister Jan and how I valued her friendship.

After a long pause I said, 'I walked here today, I wanted to feel the difference of how I am now. I saw the flowers in the church garden and the different things along the way that have become so familiar.'

After a pause Nini asked, 'What are you thinking?'

'Mam is dead six years. I was thinking how very proud she would be of me.'

With a little sigh, after a long pause, I said: 'I have been chattering!'

'I wouldn't call it chattering. You have been sharing very deeply: perhaps you sometimes mistake it for chattering, you would not have been accustomed to talking like this as a child.'

'Yes, and sometimes I am surprised and embarrassed! I wanted to bring you some flowers, instead I've brought you some flowers in a picture.' Nini received the painting with thanks and then said: 'I've got something for you, too.' Standing, she handed me a copy of her book that she had signed; the book that had made me wake up, take notice and begin to trust her!

'Good-bye and thank you,' I said, so simply, and gave her a big hug.

'Good-bye, go well and write to me.'

I went out through the red door and up the little stone steps, touching the balustrade in farewell, and went down the street with tears streaming down my face: heartbroken, but whole and alive.

Two weeks later I left for America and, astonishingly, it is already almost three years since my arrival. Life here has given me much I had hoped for and there have been some unexpected rewards in this new assignment. I am privileged to share the lives of people whose zest for life brings heightened admiration for those who bear the title 'senior citizens'. My life is enriched and inspired by the quality of their wisdom which they willingly share and by the abundance of their love, lavishly poured out from very generous hearts.

I live and work in the most beautiful of states. Early in the morning and in the quiet of the evening, in the place I now call home, deer come down from the surrounding hills into our grounds, and the smell of pine trees permeates the air with a wondrous fragrance, and the sun shines from the very highest of blue skies, so reminiscent of Africa.

Storms and flooding touch our lives frequently as predicted. Sometimes these elements hit unexpectedly and leave us floundering a while in their wake. Just so in my inner life, but the 'warm clothes' Nini prayed I might have are available each time; once I remember to wait patiently for things to change, as I have been taught, and put into practice all I have learned, I can ride out the storm with a partner still at my side.

I had the joy of meeting Nini one more time in London last year, as we had planned, on two consecutive days. It had been a long two years and I had written and received the response:

'Yes, it has been a long time! Well done.'

And there was much to celebrate when we met, for it seemed I had come home. Not only to Nini, but I had been to Ireland and taken one more step along my 'open road' ... it seemed I had a family again. The time had a hint of sadness, too, it was all so short. I said I would have liked to linger a little longer with my sisters at long last. Only my brother, my twin, had still not forgiven me.

Earlier in the year Nini had invited me to join her in writing this book: a most generous and precious gift, for it has given the little girl and I time to walk hand in hand to the cliff top and to talk about all that has been. She no longer needs to go and hide, for we both live in harmony, whole and content. That I owe much to this wonderful gentle lady, whom I now call Nini, as well as friend, is unquestionably something of an understatement, for she has given me back the gift of life.

How thankful I am to those three people: Sister Jan, Dr Fernandes and my Mother General. In the absence of their support I would not have found my way to the red door; discovered the path to the 'open road' and would have been deprived of the gift of a cherished and much-loved friend.

Insights

Now and then I find I stand
To wonder still in great surprise,
At this person full of life and love,
Who somehow seemed to rise
From the shadowy figure stiff and dark
And frozen solid with icy pain,
Until a gentle warmth,
Soft as firelight in a cosy room,
Began a thawing of its own,
And with brightness and a yellow light,
Brightened the shadows,
Broke the chill,
And still went on to warm yet more
Until, there was a belief, sure and
Strong, of someone at my side,
And someone in the inside.
November 1994.

PART THREE
The paintings

1: The Dreadful House

2: The Curtain

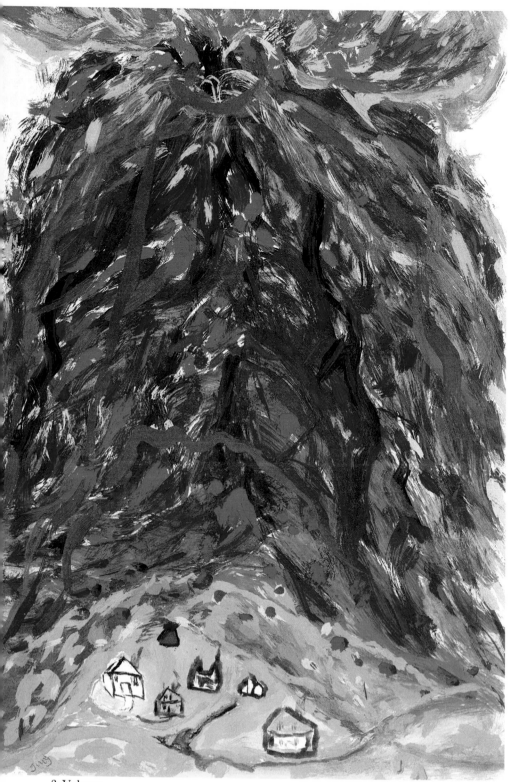

3: Volcano

4: Cliff Top

5: Country Girl

6: Drawing Closer

7: Devil Man

8: Flames: Lady in Black

9: Collage

10: Flowers Still Bloom Outside
That House

11: Children at Play

Comments on the paintings by Sister Mary

The Dreadful House

This was the very first of all the paintings and by far the most difficult to deal with. Even now, the memory of the day I drew and painted it is very vivid.

I didn't want to give up the facade of 'everything is fine – thank you', but as I drew, the picture itself seemed to take over and there emerged this tidy, contained, angry image. It was a case of the truth, but I wanted to disown it on the spot and hardly dared bring it to you.

The Curtain

This is the most frightening and most sinister of all the paintings. The emptiness, the crystal vase, the stairway door, and that curtain, chill me even now to look at them. On the day I drew it, I recall feeling sick inside and I needed to have some hot chocolate to recover. (Interesting I have made no mention of the chair: it was where my mother usually sat, beside the fire).

Volcano

The anger inside was in danger of erupting at any moment and I feared it would overflow to destroy everything. At the same time it was what I most wanted: to have the memories and that dreadful house wiped out for ever, preferably with my father buried within that awful place. To talk about that level of violence, much less to 'own' it, seemed much too dangerous – hence the painting.

Cliff Top

I felt so 'bad' and empty and wanted to be rid of the 'heartburn' feeling and all the guilt I carried. I wished I was dead and feared that one day the thought of suicide might become reality. I wanted to run away from it all – to be free.

Country Girl

I now felt a brightness and light sometimes, and slowly a growing belief in a better life, even if I still felt isolated and not good enough to live with the rest of mankind.

Drawing Closer

I sensed the little person, who came with me each time to the session, draw closer to you. It seemed safe but I was still unsure. This picture was so representative of this, yet when I brought it to you, you said it was the 'flower lady', and I noted your comment in my journal: 'but the tree has no roots'. And wrote that I was a little in awe of you, that you seemed to know without needing to be told. It would still take some time more before I could really trust you.

Devil Man

I felt so caged in by fear of this devil of a man and now, enraged by all I had endured, I had murderous feelings towards him and felt I might shoot him given the chance.

Flames: Lady in Black

It seemed there was no escape from the anger I felt. Everything in my life had been affected by it, so that it made me feel increasingly vulnerable and at risk, for I felt so very destructive. The lady in black is my twin me and Sister Jan. I had become so enraged by then, because of the memories of abuse, neglect and abandonment and felt so out of control by the level of anger, for it seemed to engulf my entire life and I feared, like the tiny girl in the picture, I would need to run and hide from all the danger that anger could cause.

Sometimes I needed to step away awhile – it seemed I might otherwise go mad – all the rage and anger would be taken, boxed, it seemed, and pushed out of my way and into Sister Jan's office. The lady's face reflects Sister Jan's dismay each time she became the recipient of some unaccountable outburst of my pent-up anger and rage.

Collage

This was a very important picture; I was, I think, beginning to take some responsibility for my life. I began to have a little understanding of what my mother had been through in her life and what a blessing the 'flower lady' had proved to be in mine, even if I felt 'displaced' once her own little girl was born.

Each image in the collage reflects the gradual awareness of the gift the lady – the 'flower lady' – had been in my life. Her memory remained in my heart and mind like some eternal barometer by which I could measure the state of things, and know always that if only I could hold on, there was good and hope. The colour – the soft yellow – I chose as a background reflects this feeling of hope.

The Rose Bowl and Yellow Rose:

A prized possession of the 'flower lady's'. I felt it an honour when she allowed me to fill it with water and select the rose each time. A trust I had known.

The Garden in a Plate:

This I helped her create and watched each time full of wonder and joy as the garden became reality: moss and stones, a tiny bridge, miniature flowers and a little lake. A creative, loving spirit.

The Crinoline Lady:

A doll she taught me to make from pipe cleaners and some lace. As we worked together, sometimes quietly, sometimes with shrieks of laughter, when the creation turned out none too beautiful and we needed to begin again. Mistakes were made but we could go on.

So that when it seemed my mother might want to kill me for what she knew I had done, still there seemed protection and someone who cared, if only I could run and stay alive long enough to find it.

Flowers Still Bloom Outside That House

Outside that house flowers still bloomed. Trees still lived and bloomed and had some flowers. The white gate to the little park is still closed but now there is a glimmer of light. I felt the dangers of that house still present, but there was a chance of life and light if only I could get away.

Children at Play

When I painted this and brought it to you, that day, I said the orphanage was a safe place where children could play and be free. My wish had sometimes been to take all five of us there, yet I so dreaded the often-stated thought to send us to that orphanage. A place of total abandonment.

Comments on the paintings by Nini Herman

When Sister Mary fell virtually silent roughly halfway through our time together, I had by that time developed certain ideas concerning the volatile contents of her inner world exploding into the transference relationship. To risk a premature interpretation, however, might have precipitated an abrupt end to her therapy, even a psychotic episode.

Besides, these flares that the unconscious threw up fluctuated at such lightning speed to suggest now an abusing father, now a murderous retaliating mother; the two at times so entangled as to convey a single combined object out to destroy her. From this death-dealing inner constellation there would be neither escape nor protection, while its ascendancy clearly threatened such vestiges of psychological health as struggled to avail against this literally 'unspeakable' hegemony.

While I experienced no small measure of Mary's own fear and intimidation projected into me during the course of her turbulent silence, I knew that if we were to get to the roots of her illness, these images that ruled her inner world, that could not be spoken, had to be extracted, defined and faced if any enduring peace of mind was to be established. It was not long after Mary had begun to paint that my hopes that we were on the right track were realised when she was able to talk about the content of her paintings sufficiently freely and with evident relief.

It struck me as interesting that while Mary's style as the author of her own story is consistently lucid, in her comments on her paintings, made some three or so years after our time together, signs of pain, of anger and of stress, even of attacks on thinking, take the language over at times. It seemed wrong to edit these residues away.

Any divergence in our respective commentaries is, no doubt, inevitable. Whereas Mary's tend to return pristine to the original here-and-now situation, my own ideas evolved in relays over many sessions and were further elaborated with hindsight in the flickering light of subsequent clinical experience.

It is interesting how my hopes that inner entanglements might be extracted and defined were in fact realised beyond expectation in that each of the painted images singled out and focused on a specific area of anxiety and conflict with surprising and edifying clarity. It was as if a housecleaner had moved in to tackle the task room by room!

Our labours carried a further bonus. This loving co-operation as equals, two explorers travelling side by side into jungle territory, with Mary often leading the way, gave us a gift of intimacy, of growing trust and of mutual respect, which it might otherwise have taken years to establish.

The Dreadful House

The first painting struck me with an icy chill that the passing of the years has certainly not diminished. I remain unable to do justice to it in words. This house is the stuff of nightmares. An obsessional control of detail conveys her childhood terror lest some dreadful secret might escape into the light of day to undermine the rigid game of 'everything is fine, thank you'.

Window curtains testify to respectability and yet no one is deceived. There are windows and a door, but no sense of 'inside' or of 'outside'. The image is two-dimensional, like the minds of autistic children, which have been described so evocatively as resembling a house where a letter posted through the front door will fall directly through the back; the mind deprived of the safety of containment which, by its nature, provides that capacious space for owning and digesting experience.[1]

This house lacks all connection with any outer world. Totally cut off, it guards some catastrophic secret. There is neither bell nor knocker since no one is expected. The letter-box is too small to receive real messages. There is no path by way of access, nothing green and nothing growing. Life is eliminated. Exit seems to be by two drainpipes either side of the bricks.[2] Those incarcerated there will never risk the light of day, know spontaneity or joy. It instils violence, disregard for all things human, loving and close. It is worse

---

[1] Mary was not autistic, but her terror, initially, froze out a third dimension.
[2] Are they symbols for parental sexuality kept apart in the child's inner world and rigidly controlled by her in phantasy?

than a madhouse because the madness is unacknowledged, cemented into the brickwork by all who enter there.

The Curtain

In her comments on this sinister picture Mary does not elaborate in detail on the curtain itself, the fact that it leads to the bedroom of her parents, that bed where sexual abuse continually took place, a first experience of which she describes in unforgettable, tormenting terms. The curtain that is the dividing line between innocence and its wanton destruction.

The shape of its black opening is that of the female genital – the opening into the vagina, hateful, ominous, bad – emblem of Greek tragedy, touching on the unbearable. In her own account it is compressed into a few lines.

But where is the crystal vase that Mary refers to so tellingly devoid of further explanation? Surely it is those three green fragments we see impaled on the wall above the television set by the explosive force of maternal fury and despair. Mary recalled how on that occasion her mother picked it up and hurled the thing against the wall, doubtless aimed at her daughter, exclaiming 'this is for broken virginity!' We felt that she must have known and colluded in the abuse. She herself was undoubtedly struggling to refuse sexual intercourse, the only means of contraception that was open to her, after her experience of puer-peral depression with its aftermath of near-psychotic episodes.

The bleakness of the room appals one. Even the flowers in the little pot are merely hinted at. They are ghost flowers. The mother's chair beside the fire looks large and cosy enough for a mother and her baby to find pleasure and comfort in. But the arms of the chair are stretched out in supplication of an occupant who is missing, a plaintiff all the more conspicuous by her absence. Only the fatal fragments adhering to the wall speak of her impotent rage, whose inner manifestation finds expression in her escape into illness, escape from the fear of her destructive feelings, flight into the mental hospi-tal where drugs will silence the rage that could not be verbalised by such a fragile, wordless persona.

Paradoxically we see a fire burning in the hearth. Mary, the 'parenting' child,[3] used to keep a fire in for her father's late return.

---

[3] A term for children who in response to parental incapacity assume the role of parent, most common with disabled mothers. If we understood this tragedy in the making we would stop praising these sacrificial victims and bestowing medals on them. We would recognise a situation in urgent need of redress – and act on it.

There the little girl would sit to await the appearance of her tormen-
tor long after the pubs had closed and her bedtime; a tragic little
replacement wife, terrified of the ordeal to come, dreading to get it
over with, the sacrifice of her child-self in a pitiful attempt to keep
father at home. If he also upped and left there was only the orphanage waiting down the cruel road, a place for waifs and unwanted
children like the ones in the street she so dreaded on her visits to
myself. There they were in all weathers, pale-faced and unkempt,
palpably unprotected, ideal subjects for projections of her trauma-
tised childhood self. Besides, might they not attack her out of envy,
the one who was receiving help?

Here I have to mention one tragic communication of hers which
belonged to that time. Almost inaudibly, it seemed to come out of the
blue: 'Even the Good Lord, my dear, would love you for your golden
hair and not yourself alone'. It had a familiar ring to it, but there was
something horribly wrong about the quotation. It was, I believed,
from a poem by Yeats. I racked my brain to recall the original
version. With much help it was tracked down.[4] The name of the
poem is 'To Anne Gregory'. The lines run: '... that only God, my
dear, could love you for yourself alone, and not your yellow hair'.
Like Mary's God, her own father was only after his own perverse
ends, oblivious of the terrible injury he thereby inflicted on his
daughter – on her nascent self.[5]

Volcano

Here, Mary's version sets the image in perspective. It is unlikely that
she could have reached that eruption of her murderous rage and
fury, bottled up for all those years, in so short a time and in such overwhelming depth, without producing that image. She would certainly
have denied it on the omnipotent assumption that it could readily
wipe out not only the parents but the entire community and, in the
transference, myself. What heroism to produce that as the other
images!

One of the tiny, helpless buildings suggests a church, her teachers,
the nuns, who failed to read her urgent, silent prayer for help.
Towards the end of our time together, Sister Mary felt strong enough
to bring her story to confession. Her father confessor threatened her
with hell and damnation and seemingly left it at that: beyond the

---

[4] Help from Danny Abse and the Poetry Library of the Arts Council.
[5] I had no occasion to explore this image of God.

pale, beyond forgiveness. Fortunately she was by then able to keep his outburst in perspective in the growing belief that she had my respect and love.

If Mary had initially hated and therefore feared the retaliating mother who had failed to protect her, who had even colluded in the abysmal situation, in time she came to suspect that 'poor Cathleen' too might well have been a victim of incest. This gradual emergence of empathy initially doubled her despair once unconscious guilt began to surface as its conscious component. Her phantasies now accused her of having failed her mother on this score as on that of her own participation in the act of incest. This development increased the persecutory image of a mother who would never love or trust her again, until in time and with relevant intervention persecution could slowly dissolve into grief and pain with the catalyst of love.

It was in the hope of transforming this paranoid maternal image, a serious obstacle to eventual reparation, that I encouraged her visit to my husband whereby 'mother' trusted her to spend time with 'father' alone, in the studio next door. As 'father' was helpful, loving and safe, this restored her earliest experience of parents who jointly further and safeguard the being of their growing child. This may well have produced the later image of 'the family' in The Collage.

Orthodox colleagues may claim that such 'short cuts' can never change the constellation of a persecutory inner world, 'bad objects into good ones'; but here I am bound to ask myself, in all honesty, whether it is always in the interests of the patient to pursue this timeless detective story as if the passing of the years was of little consequence.

Cliff Top

Thoughts of suicide had plagued Mary with a desperate sense of terror and guilt as far back as she could remember. She was dominated by a panic that if I got to hear of them I would terminate her treatment. Her fear that taking her life might become a reality rather suggests one who, at a deeper level, wants to go on living if only she knew how to escape, to 'be free' of her persecutory nightmare. If only she could discover a way of living without feeling contaminated, if at first unconsciously, by the murderous inner rage against her father and lately the entire family after her brothers and sisters rejected her.

In her painting the cliff top is gentle and green. The little stream flowing down to the sea at her feet could be tears of grief washing some of the self-hatred away in a dawning compassion for her child-self. Feelings of rage are confined to the red jumper, while the impulse to self-destruction is evoked by the wild, flying hair, the blind speed with which the child rushes towards the brink. Yet the sky, as if to negate these intentions, looks a benevolent blue, perhaps the shade associated with the all-forgiving Virgin mother's cloak.

Her own text conveys, above all, a great sense of frustration that she had so far found no way to escape from the constant sense of persecution by an abusing inner father and the ongoing complaints and accusations from a wronged inner mother, nor from that degree of self-hatred, which she defines as 'not good enough', at her own, complex part in her downfall.

Lest it be thought that I take the risk of suicide too casually, there is, in my experience, a more serious category that one might call 'inevitable'. It is a long-term, total preoccupation with compulsive ideas of self-destruction as an act of revenge and of attack on a malevolent and persecutory inner object. Mary, herself, was not in this category.[6]

Country Girl

The woman in the pretty dress who looks welcoming and kind is, on one level, a helpful aspect of myself, but also represents the 'flower lady' who with her loving support facilitated the child's crucial inner and later actual escape from the 'dreadful house'. Mary, no doubt yielding to her father's imposition of silence under dire threats, as to her sense of shame, was not able to confide her troubles to this friend, but there is little doubt in my mind, as indeed in her own, that the experience of this good mother figure was taken into her inner world to sustain her capacity for love, alongside the hateful, destructive feelings, to prevent her total disintegration.

In time, I became increasingly identified with this 'good object' on Mary's journey back to an aspect of her own good early mother. If her mother was initially spoken of as abandoning and 'mad', we now began to hear of a mother who would sew and knit beautiful things for her children, who was creative in a thousand little ways. And it was then, roughly halfway through our time together, that Mary brought me a Christmas present of a lovely shawl she had crocheted herself, in identification with this mother and with my

[6] Nini Herman (1991). Prodromal states of suicide. Thoughts on the death of Ann France. Free Associations Journal 2(2), No 22: 249–58.

creativity. She knew of my books, had read some of them, and also valued the creative contribution I had made towards her recovery which she could begin to believe in around this time.

In the painting, she is still on the other side of a formidable fence but the gate is open and a path leads to the 'flower lady's' home at a safe distance from her own, red one, perhaps incinerated by her rage.

The scene is one of spring. There are flowers everywhere. Trees are in new leaf. The sky is gentle and blue in contrast to flames and smoke over The Volcano. We see an inner world showing signs of resolution even if there remains much work to be done, as aspects of the next painting show. But then we expect two steps forward, one step back in such a prodigious task.

Drawing Closer

This is a lovely image. In this embrace we see the 'flower lady' and myself rolled into one, even if Mary's memory is right that I did not say so. With regard to the roots of the tree, it certainly *has* roots and I rather think that I would have suggested that it is not rooted in the earth.

This is where the problem concerning trust comes in. Mary certainly had roots carried over from her earliest childhood. But when her mother was taken ill and hospitalised repeatedly, in other words when she 'left her' and the abuse began, she would have pulled them up, so to speak, and waited for new, good and safe soil to replant herself as she was now beginning to do and, what was more, to own that this was happening.

I often think of this situation in terms of Christmas-flowering hyacinths. The bulbs, bought in September, have tiny little wisps of rootlets curled underneath the bulb. If one sets them in a glass jar, the water level half an inch below the bulbs, and leaves it in a dark place, within a matter of weeks the roots will begin to reach thirstily towards the water until at the end of something like six weeks they are long and strong and almost fill the jar by the time the green tips appear. In human beings it takes longer and involves a lot of pain!

While the embrace of the little girl and the 'good mother' is very touching, those free-floating roots convey something fundamentally hopeless and unresolved. It was found to rest on new aspects of the persecutory relationship to myself now, as the wronged mother, damaged and made sick by her child depriving her of father's legitimate support.

The enormous amount of black hair, when Sister Mary's is brown, underlines a mood of dark depression rooted in a dawning insight on the part of Mary that her child-self was not the only victim of sexual abuse, of incest. Like others in her situation she found it initially unbelievable and then unbearably painful to permit an image of her mother, as the other party deeply wronged, to filter into her inner world with the delayed acceptance of her parents as the rightful sexual couple.

At this stage the original depression implanted by the murderous rage at having been demeaned was compounded increasingly by feelings of guilt that now emerged at a conscious level, with her growing understanding of the above considerations that underlay her pervading sense of unworthiness, the sense of hopelessness, of 'not being good enough'.

This, I believe, returned to the fore at the stage in her therapy when Mary began to embrace a tragic inevitability in her disastrous experience. She came to understand how, with her emotionally incapacitated mother, she had no option but to turn for love and attention to her father, who took perverse advantage of her need so that she had, to that extent, been conscripted as an active partner in her despairing bid to retrieve the well-being and love of her earlier childhood. She was a victim in a dual sense, namely her father's and her needy child-self's own.

This dynamic was further complicated in that this hard-bought 'attention' paradoxically made her feel 'special' and privileged at the very gates of hell, a view that was encouraged in that her father called the violation a 'precious secret' to preserve the compliance of one terrified of losing him. For then, would she not find herself abandoned to a murderous mother or, as she always dreaded, homeless, cast into the nearby orphanage?

As a cruel epilogue to her misery, her siblings, having intuited her 'special status' with father, tended to use her influence with him in gaining their own ends in some controversy.

As in the case of Mary, where a girl senses a collapse in the parental relationship, she may, trapped in her urge to satisfy a welter of oedipal phantasies, be bewitched into the role of accomplice. Here, it will take an abusive father to translate phantasy into stark reality by taking advantage of her plight.

Devil Man

'Drawing Closer', for all its ambivalence, but by introducing an element of reconciliation with the mother, would have engendered sufficient inner security and 'ego strength' to enable Mary to express her fear and rage against the 'devil man'. This she would have had to deny while she saw herself as a motherless child and to repress in her therapy as long as I, in the transference, represented this monster! For how, while she attacked me as the abandoning mother, could she possibly afford to be at war with both parents all of the time? Besides, she felt that as a nun she must not harbour angry feelings.

This figure was undoubtedly her father and it was around this time that she had a dream in which he was burned to cinders in the conflagration of a warehouse, as had recently taken place near her home-town.

It is interesting how, with her rage surfacing as a topic for discussion, it no longer blackens her hair. Subsequent images show its natural shade of brown as the dark depression engendered by her murderous feelings, as now by her guilty feelings, begins to lift.

Mary is depicted behind bars to protect herself against the 'devil father' and the retaliating mother, still myself at times in the transference; but also to protect the 'good me' against her destructive self, still feared to be all-powerful.

At the same time she is also running away, escaping, as she had been unable to do as a child with nowhere to go; while perhaps, with another 'good' part of herself that was beginning to develop a capacity for maternal self-protection, she is running to myself who was by then seen as helping her to change. In due course, she would come to see that 'running away' in any other direction was not an ultimate solution but a denial of her good dependency needs. In the treatment it took something like two years before she began to believe that she and I – mother and daughter – had a capacity, a right and ability, to protect ourselves within a loving alliance.

This was not yet the case in the episode where my basement consulting room had suffered a break-in. With glass all over the floor, too terrified to mention the obvious disarray, she feared that her attacks on myself in the transference, following the separation of a recent break, had produced this result.

Patients who were stronger at the time commented with varying degrees of ease on the damage. For Mary, the broken glass further symbolised the shattering intrusion into her small body by the 'devil man'.

The missiles hurled at the devil man before she runs away suggest faeces and urine, the infant mind's main weaponry. As her rage now begins to be owned, her own dress is blue and no longer rage-red as on the cliff top. There, self-destructive impulses still offered the only escape from so much hatred, which had, for so long, to be denied.

The red devil man is also filled with rage that his victim is escaping to spill the beans. It struck us both as deeply sad that when, in her despair, she confided in her siblings, thereby exposing herself to the 'devil man's' wrath, she gained no protection of their solidarity until on her first home leave, three years after our time together, her oldest sister, who had meanwhile also had psychotherapy, invited her to stay.

By that time 'poor Cathleen' had long since died from cancer. Although Mary wished that they might have had more time together for mourning and reparation, she recognised how healing it had been for the two of them to have accomplished a measure of that process. That it could have been initiated before psychotherapy began is touching proof of how strong the drive for love is under the most daunting circumstances.

Before we reflect on the next image it should be said how confusing at this stage the co-existence of destructive and reparative drives, the advent of love and the coming to terms with hate and guilt, with depression, slowly infused with mourning, inevitably prove. It is as if the inner world harboured all of these, a veritable repertoire of jacks-in-the-box. In this hurly-burly the therapist can only stand by as a vigilante, ever-optimistic with regard to a healing outcome, holding all the skeins of the tangle while declining to be rattled by signs of intermittent relapse into more primitive modes of functioning.[7]

Flames: Lady in Black

Sister Mary's own account conveys once again her eruption of rage as a recurring phenomenon. We witness yet again how 'the dreadful house' goes up in flames and hear how her own dismay that these feelings decline to abate is projected into 'her twin' Sister Jan and the 'lady in black.'

I see the woman in black, who dominates the scene in such a powerful manner, as the damaged mother whom Mary, in her phantasy, repeatedly 'got rid of' into the mental hospital with her hostile and punitive attacks for her maternal failings. These the child expe-

---

[7] In Kleinian concepts here is the struggle between the paranoid-schizoid and the depressive position.

rienced as abandonment and rejection, which stoked her fury. Once she could begin to empathise with her mother it was increasingly from her omnipotent sense of guilty responsibility for 'ditching' her that she seeks to escape in the image.

Yet while 'the terrible house' goes up in flames of stockpiles of Mary's retribution, the woman in black remarkably survives, albeit in her deep depression. Compared to the devil man she remains significantly and reassuringly intact. It was hopeful that after we had absorbed this aspect of the image we gradually began to hear of a very different mother – a creative needlewoman who loved and tended her garden. Nor should we overlook the green edge to the painting. Something growing *had* survived; there is healing in the air and reparation is a possibility.

Collage

Sister Mary's comments here put us well in her picture. It came, as she explains, at a turning point in her life, as also in our work together. She tells us how she had felt 'displaced' from her place with the 'flower lady' when the latter in due course had a baby of her own.

It would have been around this time that Mary recognised that a certain lady whom she sometimes passed in the street in fact came to see me too. She experienced it as a mighty shock to find her coming through the door on one occasion as she left: the hated twin and 'my other baby', both back again! Could that perhaps be the reason why she is the only child in the little family depicted in that scene? Has she killed off all rivals, while the little girl in the dark-red coat with yellow envy in her hair looks at that other lucky only child with inscrutable feelings? Clearly there is still a split between the 'lucky' and deprived parts of Mary's personality.

Mary lists with gratitude much of what the 'flower lady' meant to her through the years. She is ever more aware what she owes to this protector of her inner and her outer world. 'There was good and there was hope.' Do we tend to overlook that where a child in her home faces little but madness, oblivion and neglect of her most basic rights, access to a role model that offers love and sanity can just suffice in many cases to hold that young mind together to an adequate degree, biding an opportunity for a favourable intervention?

'Mistakes were made but we could go on', she puts it in her own words. It was, of course, around this time that Mary spoke of her mother in less catastrophic terms. However, in the collage, set apart in a frame, side by side with hope and goodness, we still find the murderous mother, in this context dressed in red, throwing that crystal vase at the terrified child who is running for her life. But the image is contained in the frame of her therapy and myself as the 'flower lady' in the transference. Had Mary not, heroically, 'stayed alive' long enough to find me? What was more, she had found Mother General and the sisters; above all, Sister Jan. She had found Dr Fernandes, who had brought her to my door. If, as she writes, she was beginning to 'take responsibility for her life', now at a conscious level, it was because her world had changed so significantly for the better, both within and without. She could now begin to view the 'mistakes we had made', of incest – perhaps some in our work together – in a more generous and self-forgiving light. She and I could go on to progress, to eventual self-fulfilment.

'The Collage' is so interesting because it depicts the watershed of transition from one world to another, and Mary is aware of it. The murderous inner mother is no longer spilling over to contaminate life and hope with the domination of her persecutory presence. The individual items that she lists so touchingly are icons on her road to recovery. They hold a lifelong glow in her heart.

If we look at this image in the context of the earlier ones of murderous rage and self-destruction and pause to remind ourselves of a time-span of a mere single term, a matter of a dozen weeks, it suggests that our work together of the first 18 months, which took us to the 'silent' phase, had been bearing fruit for all the inner turbulence. But for this explosive content to break cover she had, in the phase of her silence, still lacked the necessary ego-strength, as also a vocabulary for expression.

Here, we should also set on record that it was around this time that Sister Mary took charge of the fine convent garden. On occasion she would bring me quite enchanting small bouquets – gardens on a plate – breathing messages of love, a capacity for gratitude and an ever-growing trust. There were now two 'flower ladies' in her life.

Flowers Still Bloom Outside That House

What a different image, what an inner transformation from the 'dreadful house'! Gone is that ghastly isolation of a house hung in space, of a catastrophic nightmare. Now it is a terraced house in a warm shade of red. It is the house in the middle like the child depicted in the previous family. It is a home, and contained, 'holding hands' with its neighbours.

That 'flowers still bloom' does suggest vividly an awareness at a deeper level that the good sense of safety now flowering in her life had carried over from her early past, and I took each opportunity to try to make this somewhat clear. As I did so, steadily, the image of her own mother took on 'the child's' respect and love and a deeper understanding of her mother's difficulties. The child was being restored to her own early mother, who had once been 'good enough'.

In the course of our time together, the image of Mary's father underwent little change. That could be asking too much. But in my husband, Josef, Mary gained the experience of a good and loving father and it is my belief that this neutralised and outweighed to an important extent the destructive and persecutory power of the 'devil man'. It may still bear fruit.

There is, of course, still her sentence, 'if only I could get away'. And yet her actual life suggested how fast she was now achieving this, not in terms of an escape but a welcome progression of inner change. Before she herself recognised this transformation I heard from her time and again how her community was delighted with her evident progress. She no longer hid away at social functions. She played her guitar and sang for the congregation, as she had previously to the sheer delight of children back in Africa, before she finally broke down. We now had to focus on aspects of inner prohibition to let her own awareness of solid progress grow and for her life to take root in that inner affirmation. Nor should we overlook these flowering trees which *are* rooted!

But delaying this awareness of growing confidence and strength there were still guilty feelings: did she deserve to go free along what we called the 'open road'? Could she really have a life so much richer than her mother's, come to know inner peace, or had she maybe stolen mine; classical anxieties on the path to recovery furthered by 'concrete thinking'?

Children at Play

While I studied this image I had to bide my time for Sister Mary's own comments on it to reach me from across the Atlantic. I, myself, could only see five happy children: herself, and her siblings, restored to loving unity, and certainly had no idea that this flowery scene represented the orphanage, a place of dread.

In her comments Mary here intuits an area of sinister defusion between the life and death instincts. 'To take all five of us there' would, in fact, have presented no viable, life-affirming solution but a cop-out, an idealisation of a sick and self-defeating status quo; a manic quest for sanctuary where the sinister reality was lost that the orphanage represented a return to total abandonment; a tragic terminus on her brave road to search for help and health.

How interesting that this conclusive phase of her paintings should, in her own words, foreshadow her eventual understanding that the final resolution of her illness would rest on her capacity to differentiate good from evil in its deceptive guises.

This, of course, is not to claim that orphanages are evil, despite all the devastating tales of abuse that are steadily coming to light. But for her – this courageous warrior in her quest for coming home to her true, good self, in other words for healing – the painful and joyful labour of sorting truth from falsehood, self-deceit and psychological squalor from the upright stance of holding out for inner truth, was not to be jettisoned. Put in her own words, it was a case of reaching out for 'being a fully fledged, thinking, feeling, loving member of the human race which is grand, wonderful and terrible too'.

Mary enlarged on this understanding in her subsequent letters wherein she described the new experience of 'roller-coaster' feelings to which she was now open and at the same time vulnerable. Grief, at the death of new friends and of people in her care; the joy of ever-new friendships with their opportunity to love generously and freely, with her great capacity for giving love still growing as she travels her open road.

She does not in the course of her story acknowledge and take credit for the strength of her determination to live against all the odds. How heroic her impressive stand against her father to leave school prematurely. Although she regretted it in the obvious sense, part of her true self which had remarkably survived in some secret shelter recognised the need to break his stranglehold and to begin, quite alone, to strike out on a life, that, still hidden in the mists of time, was to become her own. It was this spark in her personality that helped us so remarkably on our way.

Hopefully, too, we have together made a case for combining art therapy and classical, rigorous, analytical psychotherapy with a single therapist so as not to split the transference.

Nini Herman: Reflections

As Sister Mary's chapters reached me in instalments from across the Atlantic, she was offering me an unusual gift – a mirror-image of myself as a psychotherapist – one in which I could recognise myself clearly. I had, by then, already received a number of letters telling me of her new life with that touching heartfelt simplicity, such crystal-clear straightforwardness, where it is easy to trust each experience as if it was entirely one's own. And so, as I looked into that mirror, I could confirm that what I was seeing through the eyes of her memory was a totally honest unrolling of our time together, delighted by the minimum of idealisation.

Already, as we studied her paintings and as this collaboration enabled her to reach levels of hurt and later joy at quite breathtaking speed, I intuited creative gifts that came straight from the heart, as all true creativity must. And it was, I rather think, that when she referred to Terry Waite's recent autobiography at some time in our second year, that I read into these statements a passionate yearning that she, too, might find her way into the treasure house of her own full creative potential. Hence my instant response then whether she might not like one day to write her own, the story of her life.

A therapist's contribution must surely differ from patient to patient. Each is a unique being ultimately offering up the fabric of a soul's drawn-out struggle to come into its own from a lifetime in hiding, of battling with the longing and the fear of being known, of running that tremulous risk unlike any other we are likely to run in our short time on earth. And it strikes me, more fully, as the months since working on our project run by, how exceptional that soul of hers must be to have drawn from me, in my turn, responses – the like of which I have not been drawn into before.

Yes, I had already for a long time run a mile from presenting myself as what I call 'the faceless analyst'. And this is perhaps the

place at which to try to clarify somewhat the nature of my objection
to that phenomenon as it hurt me so painfully in my own experience
as an analysand and continues to hurt me deeply – for all the significant and complex benefit that I derived and all the undisputed
growth that I was helped to achieve.

Struggling even now to define my horror – that is still my only
word for this fabrication – it boils down, I believe, to that 'technique'
by which the adult part of the patient is wiped out, in that reality is
pushed aside in exclusive favour of the infant's inner world of phantasy, which is regarded as the only material fit for interpretation: a
humiliating and disorientating experience.

Here, it might help to give a fictitious example. A patient arrives
at a session and sees that the analyst's car has clearly been involved in
an accident since there is indisputable evidence of damage. Anxious
comments will meet with: 'Perhaps, after the separation of the recent
break you feel you have attacked me as the sexual parents who went
off, forgetting all about you.' Or, 'you always wanted my wife dead so
that you could marry me', and more of the same.

What adds insult to injury is that these 'intrusions' from the couch
are interpreted in that chilling tone of voice which an adult reserves
for a difficult child. Here is a discourse where the Kleinian cosmol-
ogy wipes out any validation of the analysand's hard-won perception
of reality, of discriminating truth from strategy.

By contrast, I – having dwelled on and examined deeper issues,
even perhaps psychotic anxieties in a package of communication
presented as reality – will add: 'But of course, your perceptions are
also based on reality and this we must never forget or we may lose
sight of the adult part of yourself', or words to that effect.

Every patient comes to us on the run from psychic pain, lost in a
web of strategies. We can almost assume that double-binds, that
innuendoes, a serious incapacity for mothering, for parenting, for
containing the inchoate psyche's bid to trust its orientation in the
new, extra-uterine environment, lie at the root of damage to the
heuristic instinct, the ability to learn to sift reality from phantasy, fact
from fiction. To then meet in this painful struggle for sanity with
more of the same ineluctable confusion is to undo a whole measure
of trust, of belief in this new terra firma, that has so slowly been built
up over a period of time. I have, on occasion, in my own analysis,
fought tearfully until the cows come home for one sentence that
acknowledges that I am not crazy as, thrown by these proceedings, I
may well still fear, but can trust my perceptions.

We can see, for instance, in Sister Mary's tale, how she still had to ignore the reality of broken glass and disarray in my consulting room after a break-in. How important I felt it was that, as well as looking at her deeper anxieties – that she herself, or an abusing father had caused the destruction – I then pointed out the *facts* of the disturbance, to her enormous relief and, yes, progress!

In her story, she refers to my telephone call after I had been deeply moved by an interview on television with Maya Angelou[1] after she had read a work of hers, commissioned for the occasion, on Capitol Hill for the inauguration of President Clinton. She had previously made it known that, as a child, she had been sexually abused by her father, and, I believe, had remained mute for a number of years. The interview had filled me once again with that old sense of excitement that all things are possible in the realm of human growth despite the most wretched soil of that child's beginning. That it is never too late to have a happy childhood. But for this incredible reprieve to take place, the therapist has, for the time needed to heal, to be the honest, straightforward parent that the child did not, initially, have.

In cases where the therapeutic process mounts such a rescue operation, the child in that patient will have been restored to such aspects of the early parents as were good enough, while the newly integrated adult part of the personality may well have come to terms with their failings, this newly won compassion rooted in trust and love for their therapist.

But it may not always be possible. For although we heard Sister Mary speak sympathetically of her father's very real difficulties as a single parent, she has remained unable – so far – to make her peace with that hard-pressed man who, from when she was six, had hurt her so grievously, perhaps unforgivably, over a number of years.

It meant that we were up against an inner father who remained dangerous and hateful, as well as a mother who could never trust father and daughter not to repeat those terrible scenes that had annulled her wifehood.

It must have been on the basis of this recognition – and I have never done this before or since – that I found my way to encouraging the meeting between her and the artist who is my husband, ostensibly to discuss her paintings. Mary's account of the episode speaks for itself while it offered me a deeply moving encounter with the 'father'

---

[1] A great American poet. Author of *I Know Why The Caged Bird Sings*.

in this triangle, and the part he played in her recovery. I can vouch that there is no idealisation in her recollection of the event. Josef's door is always open to students, fellow artists, to one and all who come to bask in his warmth and wisdom to go away nourished and sustained. But I had never before, or since, called on him for that particular purpose.

For a therapist to work in this manner, integrating the spontaneous within the context of a classical therapy, will be said to throw the process out in a reckless manner. The risk is that it will mobilise a flood of manic defences, of infantile omnipotence, i.e. 'I must be very special', or increase the erotic content of the transference; or the patient may even be swept into the quagmire of delusions, a break with reality.

Mania and omnipotence to a florid degree are not universal factors. Margaret Little, as far as we can judge, did not fall victim to these when Winnicott in the fifth and final year of her analysis – putting into practice his theory of 'regression to dependence' – escorted her for the duration of that summer break to a hospital of his choice, and later fetched her back again.

Should we not remind ourselves that the plunge into delusion, a psychotic transference, will hardly come out of the blue? As we grow to know our patient, intuition and experience will have helped to orientate us in the lie of the inner land; how far the sickness is contained by a degree of health.

Where psychotic proclivities exist these will have thrown up their flare here and there along the roadside, harbingers in the dark. Furthermore, I myself do not treat psychotic patients. I know my limitations. One experience was enough. That, of course, does not rule out psychotic anxieties in a more straightforward case.[2] But where we have misjudged our ground, finding ourselves up against unforeseen turbulence in a subsequent encounter, this can then be taken up and often not without advantage.

My 'unruly' interventions in Sister Mary's case did not come from a 'psychotherapist', but from the heart of a mother, the soul of a loving friend, and as such, to judge by her account, they were surely woven into her recovery.

We do not heal only by what we know, but primarily by what we *are*, above all through truthfulness and courage, the gift of spontaneity. I can never forget reading how, when Winnicott was taken ill with a coronary in a session with Margaret Little, she said: 'You must go home. This is a coronary.' He made no interpretation. On his return to work he said: 'You were right. It was a coronary.'

---

[2] Many analysts would maintain no such thing exists.

But neither the pathways followed with Sister Mary, nor the happy outcome, should be seen as a panacea. If her religious community saw it as something of a miracle, then it needs to be pointed out that there were distinct advantages at the starting post of her life, as all along the time-span of our journey.

Since she had clearly enjoyed a loving and secure early childhood until the breakdown of her mother, the outcome of our work ultimately rested on Mary being restored to the arms of a good early mother: no run-of-the-mill opportunity.

Second, we had the benefit of the steady support from a wise and loving, a quite exceptional Mother General. By the time she broke down and a serious search for help began, thanks to the insight of Dr Fernandes, Mary had been a member of that sisterhood for a quarter of a century, showing herself as one who brought special gifts to her vocation. For these she was valued and loved. Neither may we forget the staunch presence of her friend Sister Jan and the comfort of her faith; in other words, the benefits which many of our secular patients lack. [3]

So far, so good. It all sounds rather nice and cosy – as if the two of us got on like the proverbial house on fire! What pitfalls have I overlooked? What finesse of the obligatory proceedings have I evaded to lay myself open to rebuke? Or, as we shall shortly see, what other factors are involved?

Since the earliest days of Freud, the subject of sexual child abuse, which is more prevalent even today than we want to know, has appalled not only society at large, but also the professionals who are delegated to treat the aftermath in later adolescence or young adulthood.

We must remind ourselves that Freud himself, convinced at the outset of his marathon in probing the unconscious that the cases of hysteria he was treating at the time had their origin in sexual abuse in early childhood, was forced to choose between staying with his discovery or having his professional prospects dashed, rendering him penniless – a prospect that as a respectable, conscientious breadwinner, he dreaded most – or drawing the veil over this truth and to 'turn his back on his patients and the reality of their traumatic experiences'. [4]

Let those who attack Freud for that volte-face not forget that, even in this day and age of the so-called permissive society, where

---

[3] Sister Mary never raised the subject of her religious belief so that I had no occasion to take it up.

[4] Felicity de Zulueta (1993). *The Traumatic Roots Of Destructiveness*. From Pain to Violence. London: Whurr Publishers, p140.

behaviour once deemed totally unacceptable, indeed, punished by
ostracism, boasts brash credentials, incest between father and
daughter, as sexual abuse in general, would seem to be that last big
offence on our statute book of morals. Are there not psychiatrists
who, confronted by an unspeakable and unspeaking woman patient,
so that they smell a rat, still tend to resort to punitive regimes: drug
treatments that reduce the patient to a zombie, and/or the dreaded
electro-convulsive therapy?

These unfortunate patients are said to evoke terror and disgust,
pushing their rage, their sadism and seductive proclivities down the
psyche of those whom society pays to sort them out. This, I cannot
dispute. In sessions of stormy seas I cling to the mast of my certainty
that in such a deeply split personality there is also a good self, time
and again overwhelmed by waves of trauma that was endured in a
night of helpless isolation. Let it not be thought that Mary and I did
not encounter, even evaded, these dark nights of the soul.

In her book, Felicity de Zulueta illustrates psychiatry and
psychotherapy in action in their most culpable and inept form by
citing the case of 'Rachel'. An incest victim, she comes across rather
like a wild and dangerous animal who should be behind bars in the
zoo. From the age of 17 to 22, Rachel had an agonisingly chequered
career as a psychiatric patient. Written off with every diagnostic label
under the sun, including paranoid schizophrenia, she was in and out
of hospital for five years of her young life. Then, in fragments of her
own story, we read touchingly, 'the day I (finally) embarked on
analytical psychotherapy was the first day of the coming to realisation of my true self identity ... I had at last found someone who
wanted to work with me, wanted to hear me, even with the risk that
both myself and the therapist involved knew that a very painful and
bumpy road lay ahead of us.' [5]

But what happened next when that tiny spark of hope had been
kindled? That first therapeutic contract was confined to 18 months!
Even if Rachel had sent out those first, tentative feelers of hope, the
brevity of the arrangement inevitably precluded any mention of
incest, lest even that meagre lease of support be abruptly terminated
– the constant dread of these patients, who are all too aware that a
therapist–companion on their journey to healing may well be put
through unacceptable pain and even anguish.

---

[5] Ibid, p. 143.

With Rachel still reeling from her premature abandonment of this initial endeavour, her supportive psychiatrist found her another therapeutic contract, this time one session per week for six months. While this, we are told, produced valuable long-term gains leading to marriage and a creative life in music and writing, the process of the actual treatment reads like a chapter from El Niño as we hear of its havoc wrought in the tropics!

At this point I have to return to the question whether my having avoided the lurid pitfalls of Rachel's once-a-week therapist could be put down to evasive tactics on my part where deeper issues were concerned or to some other aspect of the 'technique' and setting having been handled in a neglectful or culpable manner. It is surely a significant question to raise and to attempt to answer.

My first reply to how the excruciating experiences and events for both partners, as described in the case of Rachel and elsewhere in the literature, are to be mitigated, is that the treatment of these and most other patients needs to be open-ended.

Second, that the frequency of the sessions in each week inevitably plays a significant part where so much mistrust, rage and pain have ultimately to be faced rather than aborted and/or acted out.

With only a single weekly session, psychoanalytical psychotherapy can be compared to surgery without general anaesthetic. We all know how much we long for the first post-operative visit from our surgeon where bodily interventions are concerned. We want our mind to be set at rest that all went well or that we can expect to survive unwelcome news and complications. If, on the other hand, we are left to mull over our phantasies and misgivings alone for days on end, perhaps even for an entire week, we would be entitled to consider such proceedings as malpractice. In this context, is offering the incest victim a solitary session per week not, in itself, a repetition of psychological abuse? Is it really surprising that Rachel, at times, had an overwhelming impulse to hit her therapist who, instead of interpreting her legitimate outrage, threatened to terminate the treatment on any such occurrence. For Rachel, 'caring and abuse had become intimately linked for this young woman'.[6]

There is no doubt in my mind that the four- or five-times-a-week sessions of open-ended psychoanalysis and therapy take much heat and distress out of the process. Not only is pain and the impact of

---

[6] Ibid, p.147.

childhood memories, which are erupting and exploding into the here-and-now of transference and of consciousness, contained more readily but the crucial issue of separation anxiety can be tackled from the outset. Already after the initial week of such a process the first weekend break will introduce the despairing hostility and mistrust of abandonment that turns the therapist, a potentially good object, into a thoroughly bad one. It means that this issue, central to laying down a bedrock of trust, can be addressed and worked through from the very beginning, drawn-out rehearsal to meet the flare-up, the full sound and fury at the termination of treatment which both parties will have agreed on together many months before the last session arrives. The patient here, on familiar ground with that issue, will hopefully be in a position to pull through this crucial struggle to long-term well-being.

In terms of reality this luxury cannot be widely available. So what is to be done to help the growing numbers of victims coming to light? When I said that in her own story Sister Mary offered me a mirror image of myself as a psychotherapist, one of which, on the whole, I approved, how do I justify this response?

After all, we had to make do with only two sessions per week. We could certainly appreciate warmly that Mother General's permission for the second weekly session was already a miracle. We were, after all, in her hands. That she then, once she could recognise steady progress, gave us the gift of open-ended time was ground for celebration. Gratitude out-weighed serious resentment of restriction as Sister Mary loved and trusted her Mother General.

As far as my role was concerned, I have only intermittent doubt that my heartfelt, spontaneous interventions went a long way to furthering trust in the growing realisation that, for all the inevitable setbacks, there would be daylight at the end of a long tunnel. Does Sister Mary not tell us how, after I had telephoned her one evening to share with her my joy at seeing Maya Angelou, she felt that 'there was now someone with me in that terrible house'? Do we not hear repeatedly of her growing feeling 'that there was somebody there for me'? Would we have reached these heart-warming landmarks along the orthodox route: no smiles, no responses to her hug in so relatively short a time?

Let me here, for a moment, divert to a phase of my apprenticeship, when I worked in a therapeutic community in a mental hospital. The patients there had suffered every kind of dehumanisation in early life. Today, I have little doubt that sexual abuse was part of the package they had brought with them, even if a quarter of a century ago this diagnosis never emerged.

They were divided into three 'small groups' of six to eight patients per group and treated with traditional group therapy by three of us. In the course of my three or four years of employment I cannot now recall any spectacular progress among the patients. One, indeed, absconded and killed herself; another was so continuously cutting himself that the outlook seemed grim. But one patient could leave the unit much improved, which should have merited serious reflection.

As she was in my group, the night staff called me late on one occasion. Jean, they said, was acting out, was disturbed and causing disturbance all around. Could they increase her sedative medication? I said that I was coming over.

The young woman, who had formerly been a nurse, was clearly in great distress. She was convinced that she had killed her parents. I took an unusual step, later much disapproved of by my colleagues. We got in my car and drove the few miles to her parents' council house. They were still up over a last pot of tea. The two of us enjoyed our share and Jean, greatly reassured, had a good night with no need for medication. The cycle of dehumanisation, if not broken, had received a substantial crack!

It could, of course, be argued that, as far as I know, she was not, in fact, a victim of sexual abuse but of other, unacknowledged trauma. Again, I believe passionately that group therapy cannot reach the roots of a truly catastrophic start to life.

My own journey through psychotherapy began as a group patient of the Tavistock Clinic when it was still situated in Beaumont Street in the West End of London. One or two of the patients had been attending for years and seemed considerably worse off than myself. As a doctor I became the subject of envy and hostility. I do not recall that this was interpreted. I absconded.

When I said that I approved of the mirror-image of myself as a psychotherapist that Sister Mary offered me, it enabled me to reassure myself that I remained an ordinary, loving human being without strategies. When she gave me a hug I responded. When she needed the occasional telephone call, it was on offer and responded to. And when we were clearly stuck, we changed tactics, had our term of art therapy, and moved closer to her 'open road'.

Resources, as we all know only too well, are ever more limited. Open-ended five times a week analytical psycho-therapy is simply not available in the N.H.S. and hard to finance even in the private sector. Is this not all the more reason to explore the path that Sister Mary and I followed? Can we really subscribe to growing numbers of Rachels where treatment serves to multiply distress unnecessarily?

The immediate objection here will be the substantial investment in training that would be envisaged. I believe that we are wrong, terribly wrong, to make a university degree a pre-condition for acceptance to a training in psychotherapy. (I shall never forget how upset Josef was when art schools stipulated two A levels for admission. 'Van Gogh would never have passed his,' he mourned!)

Patients, like Sister Mary, basically suffer from a broken heart. They cannot believe that anyone could ever love them, want them, or other than despise them as they despise themselves. They need to be 'nursed' out of a wretched lack of self-esteem, self-hatred, inability to believe in their good self, their loving feelings in the face of their (narcissistic) rage, with its tantrums of murderous hostility evoked by disappointment, frustration and let-down, imagined and real.

Such 'nurses' exist in the wider population, often without owning their gift. Sister Mary's 'flower lady' was one. She held that child's quaking mind together, thereby preventing a collapse into more serious illness, a break with reality.

They have existed throughout time and in every culture. Theirs is the gift of the open heart that no amount of training can inculcate or ultimately destroy, one that enables such a 'therapist' (we can all recognise them in the occasional hospital nurse, social worker and tea-lady) to avoid the pitfalls inherent in a rigid, studied agenda, since heart and mind are part of the same reality that Buddhists call 'the big mind'.[7] Surely a suitable training in 'healing relationship' could be devised to swell their number and equip them with the necessary skills, above all an experience and grasp of the works of the unconscious, something that may not be a part of the present training in counselling.

'Do-gooders' can do untold damage to their patients and to themselves. Such a training would certainly include a period of analytical psychotherapy, an experience in art therapy followed by prolonged (group) supervision of clinical work. The project would need to be subsidised. But in the long run the benefits would outweigh the investment in securing generations against patterns of trauma being handed down and perpetuated.

In this context, one of generations and their downfall, could anything further be extrapolated concerning the illness of Mary's mother, of 'poor Cathleen'? To say the least, we are here confronted

---

[7] John Welwood (1985). *Introduction to Awakening The Heart. East and West Approaches To Psychotherapy and the Healing Relationship*. Shambala, Boston & London.

by a number of mysteries. Why did Mary, the child, only discover by accident that her mother's father had spent a significant part of his life in St Josef's, that place in which his daughter, Cathleen, sought refuge repeatedly? No grandfather figures in Mary's glowing report of her early years in her grandparents' home. She stumbled on this maternal grandfather (where was the paternal one?) in the saddest circumstances, but without speculating in depth on the part this might have played in her mother's as in her own identification with madness, in the sorrows of this human chain.

Might 'Nanna', in her semi-widowhood, not have clung to her daughter in a merged and entangled relationship, a symbiotic bond breached so abruptly at an inopportune moment when the latter found herself 'stranded' under her own roof, pregnant with a fifth unwanted pregnancy and with a husband whose own background of difficulties we can only surmise in a seeming lack of closer family ties as in his abuse of Mary. A husband who, when we hear of 'loud music' and 'maternal sobs' in Mary's story, was hardly a man to reflect on the effect of his sexual appetite on a fragile wife who, in the prevailing absence of contraception, must have lived in terror of yet another pregnancy; who furthermore, poor soul, evidently aware of Mary's, her child's, suffering, was unable to come to her rescue; as to that of her own defeated child-self.

It is hardly surprising that once Mary's parents had separated her mother gained some equanimity until she developed breast cancer and died from it. This sketch in outline with so much missing data leaves us in little doubt that 'poor Cathleen's' history was weighted for defeat from her earliest years and how that defeat in its turn inevitably undermined Mary.

Here, one is bound to reflect how a little girl whose early years of childhood were happy, as she describes so vividly, only fell victim to abuse once the family situation had suffered prolonged crisis in tragic isolation.

In other words, it is only in the defeated family – one that has almost certainly been in the making for generations – that the 'psychological immune system', so to speak, breaks down in all parties to produce the susceptibility for dehumanisation to proliferate into its extreme forms to include incest, among other manifestations. A similar sequence of events no doubt affects societies and nations where exceptional hardship and, above all, armed conflict and war are the historical springboard for wider dysfunction; surely a cogent reason for the international community to intervene more swiftly and effectively where these long-term catastrophes are brewing. Likewise we are slow to learn that the social microcosm requires watchdogs, less overworked than its spearheads are today, so that they stand alert to intervene meaningfully once a red light appears.

How clearly we hear Sister Mary in the telling of her story rage and grieve over how no one, absolutely no one, seemed prepared or able to read the signs that were surely loud and clear in their plea for prompt action, for a deeper understanding of her tragic predicament.

In the same grievous context Sister Mary also provides a lamentable and convincing picture of the painfully unguided stages through which those of us who teeter on the brink of collapse from paralysing anxieties and crippling conflict, those who can neither live nor die, seek every subterfuge to escape from that realisation – from the urgency of their need to lay aside 'rose-tinted spectacles' of denial to go in search of skilled professional help. How it can consequently take half a lifetime, or longer, of suffering to undo the knack of keeping our ailment under lock and key.

How plangently Mary describes how 'I was seriously ill but I still tried to hide it from myself', while those around her at the time, well-intentioned as they were, kept leading her to 'patchers-up'.

In the event Mary was finally fortunate that, in finding Dr Paula Fernandes, she knocked on the door of one of those all-too-rare members of the medical profession with a deep understanding that widely different categories of help are needed for widely different varieties of psychological distress. That neither anti-depressants nor 'pep' pills, so readily resorted to by hard-pressed family doctors; nor 'therapies' that side-step the unconscious; can, in the long run, alleviate degrees of suffering, of profound malfunction, that lead to a wasted life or to suicide.

When I was a medical student during the war, the name of Freud was never mentioned. Psychoanalysis and its offspring psychoanalytical psychotherapy, and their potential for benefit, did not exist in any lecture we attended nor any textbook of psychiatry. That gap still requires urgent redress. Societies that we call 'primitive', within their cultural givens concern themselves more searchingly with problems of the wandering human spirit.

While we find that the echelons of science still tend to launch missiles of ridicule and abuse at psychoanalysis – today a consensus of the widest range of spiritual disciplines – those that can accept the role of the unconscious – are exploring paths to a collaboration that is already bearing fruit where arid fundamentalism is increasingly recognized to be counterproductive.